Arguing from Cognitive
Science of Religion

Also available from Bloomsbury

Advances in Religion, Cognitive Science, and Experimental Philosophy,
edited by Helen De Cruz and Ryan Nichols
Debating Christian Religious Epistemology, edited by John M. DePoe
and Tyler Dalton McNabb
Free Will and Epistemology, by Robert Lockie
Philosophical Foundations of the Cognitive Science of Religion, by
Robert N. McCauley with E. Thomas Lawson
Progressive Atheism, by J. L. Schellenberg

Arguing from Cognitive Science of Religion

Is Religious Belief Debunked?

Hans van Eyghen

BLOOMSBURY ACADEMIC
LONDON • NEW YORK • OXFORD • NEW DELHI • SYDNEY

BLOOMSBURY ACADEMIC
Bloomsbury Publishing Plc
50 Bedford Square, London, WC1B 3DP, UK
1385 Broadway, New York, NY 10018, USA
29 Earlsfort Terrace, Dublin 2, Ireland

BLOOMSBURY, BLOOMSBURY ACADEMIC and the Diana logo are trademarks of Bloomsbury Publishing Plc

First published in Great Britain 2020
This paperback edition published in 2021

Copyright © Hans van Eyghen, 2020

Hans van Eyghen has asserted his right under the Copyright, Designs and Patents Act, 1988, to be identified as Author of this work.

For legal purposes the Acknowledgments on p. vi constitute an extension of this copyright page.

Cover design: Louise Dugdale
Cover image: © shaunl/Getty Images

All rights reserved. No part of this publication may be reproduced or transmitted in any form or by any means, electronic or mechanical, including photocopying, recording, or any information storage or retrieval system, without prior permission in writing from the publishers.

Bloomsbury Publishing Plc does not have any control over, or responsibility for, any third-party websites referred to or in this book. All internet addresses given in this book were correct at the time of going to press. The author and publisher regret any inconvenience caused if addresses have changed or sites have ceased to exist, but can accept no responsibility for any such changes.

A catalogue record for this book is available from the British Library.

A catalog record for this book is available from the Library of Congress.

ISBN: HB: 978-1-3501-0029-9
PB: 978-1-3502-9018-1
ePDF: 978-1-3501-0030-5
eBook: 978-1-3501-0031-2

Typeset by Deanta Global Publishing Services, Chennai, India

To find out more about our authors and books visit www.bloomsbury.com and sign up for our newsletters.

Contents

Acknowledgments		vi
Introduction: Debunking Arguments against Religious Belief		1
1	What Are Religious Beliefs, Supernatural Beliefs, and Religious Experiences?	5
2	CSR: Explaining Religious Belief	13
3	CSR: Explaining Ritual Behavior and Religious Experiences	45
4	Are CSR and Religious Belief Incompatible?	61
5	Arguing for Unreliability	81
6	Arguing for Naturalistic Religious Experiences	113
7	Arguing against the Consensus Gentium Argument	129
Conclusion		147
Notes		149
References		178
Index		197

Acknowledgments

The book is an adapted version of my research project completed at VU Amsterdam. I thank all the people who helped me in my research. Special thanks go out to my supervisors, Rik Peels, Gijsbert van den Brink, and Ren'e van Woudenberg. I also thank Lieke Asma, Leon de Bruin, Jeroen de Ridder, Naomi Kloosterboer, Scott Robbins, Emmanuel Rutten, and other colleagues at the Abraham Kuyper Center for their extensive comments on earlier drafts.

I am greatly indebted to all cognitive scientists I met for helping me understand cognitive science of religion and teaching me new ways to look at religious belief. Special thanks go out to Robert McCauley and the staff of the Center for Mind and Brain at Emory University, Atlanta, for facilitating a research leave.

I thank all the people I met during academic events who commented on my work. Although comments were often critical, they helped me sharpen my ideas and preempt counterarguments.

Final thanks go out to the people who gave moral and practical support in completing this book. I thank my parents and siblings for their support. I thank my fiancée for her support and careful proofreading of the whole manuscript.

Introduction: Debunking Arguments against Religious Belief

This book investigates whether recent theories from cognitive science of religion (CSR) support debunking arguments against religious belief. In my introduction, I briefly discuss debunking arguments in general and what my book adds to the discussion.

0.1 Debunking Arguments Abound

The term "debunking argument" rose to prominence in the debate over the impact of evolutionary explanations of morality. Biologists proposed evolutionary explanations of altruism and moral emotions.[1] They argue that moral behavior and moral emotions evolved gradually to tackle evolutionary challenges. Some authors argue that the explanations cast doubt on the truth or justification of moral beliefs.[2] Famous arguments against morality were defended by Michael Ruse and Edward O. Wilson, Sharon Street and Richard Joyce.[3] All arguments argue that the evolutionary history of moral beliefs makes it unlikely that they reflect moral truths. The arguments triggered a huge amount of responses,[4] and some counterresponses.[5]

Debunking arguments were raised in other domains as well.[6] Benjamin Libet conducted a number of studies showing that conscious decisions are preceded by neural activity.[7] Libet's research is often cited to argue that humans do not have free will. Daniel Wegner provided other neuroscientific evidence to cast doubt on belief in libertarian free will.[8] Debunking arguments against free will also triggered defensive responses.[9]

Not all debunking arguments target common-sense beliefs, like moral beliefs or belief in free will. One famous argument targets scientific beliefs. Alvin Plantinga argues that if naturalistic Darwinism is true, there is only a small chance that our belief-forming mechanisms are aimed at truth. Therefore, we should not judge the (common-sense and scientific) beliefs they produce as true.[10] While Plantinga merely uses his debunking argument to show that naturalism (the thesis that there are no supernatural beings) does not square well with science, others discussed debunking arguments against scientific beliefs in isolation.[11] To my knowledge, no author defended an argument against scientific beliefs at length.

Debunking arguments tend to refer to scientific evidence to argue that beliefs are epistemically tainted. The scientific evidence is often evolutionary biology, but need not be as debunking arguments against free will show.

0.2 Debunking Religious Belief

In this book, I discuss debunking arguments against religious belief. Religious belief has not been subject to as many attacks as moral beliefs or free will. This is slowly changing because of the growing influence of cognitive theories of religious belief. Debunking arguments against religious belief do have predecessors in the work of William James (1902) and Sigmund Freud (1961). James discussed how the religious enthusiasm of George Fox, the founder of the Quaker religion, can easily be attributed to an unsound mind. James also notes that a similar argument can be made against the antireligious temperament of some atheists. Their antireligious fervor can be attributed to bad digestion or a torpid liver.[12]

Freud argues that religious belief stems from the Oedipus complex, and ultimately from man's helplessness in the world. Belief in God stems from the need of a father figure who provides safety and relief.[13]

Some claim that little has changed since the days of James and Freud and that new debunking arguments against religious belief merely reiterate older (refuted) arguments. I disagree. The scientific theories to which new debunking arguments refer are a lot more advanced and corroborated by empirical evidence than the science that was available to James and Freud. Scientists working in the field have gathered considerable empirical data in support of their theories and draw on well-supported general theories in cognitive science. Philosophical reflection on debunking arguments has also advanced.[14] New arguments argue why bodily constitution (or rather cognitive constitution) would lead subjects *astray*. The arguments thereby move beyond simple arguments that commit the genetic fallacy. Most arguments also move beyond sweeping "nothing but" claims.

The first debunking arguments against religious belief were construed by defenders of religious belief. The aim was preempting potential challenges or responding to perceived challenges from cognitive scientists.[15] Later, new and more elaborate debunking arguments were put forward. Though they vary considerably, they all refer to new evidence from CSR to argue that religious belief is epistemically tainted.[16]

In this book, I distinguish four rather different debunking arguments. A first group of arguments argues that CSR theories make claims that are incompatible with religious belief. A second group argues that CSR theories show that religious belief is unreliably formed. Most existing debunking arguments against religious belief fall in this group. A third group zooms in on religious experiences. They argue that CSR theories give naturalistic explanations of religious experiences and thereby undo their evidential value. A final group of arguments is similar. They argue that CSR theories can undo the evidential value of religious beliefs themselves by giving naturalistic explanations.

This book is structured as follows: In the first chapter I give an analysis of the target of debunking arguments, religious beliefs. In the second and third I look closer to some of the main theories in CSR. In the fourth I critically evaluate arguments for the conclusion that CSR and religious belief are incompatible. In the fifth I evaluate unreliability arguments. In the sixth I look at the argument against religious experiences. I construe it as a counterargument against the argument *from* religious experiences. In the seventh chapter I look at the argument against the evidential value of religious beliefs themselves, which I construe as a response against the consensus gentium argument.

1

What Are Religious Beliefs, Supernatural Beliefs, and Religious Experiences?

1.1 Introduction

Before we can tackle the various debunking arguments, we need two things. We need a clear understanding of the science to which debunking arguments refer. I will work toward this in the next chapter. We also need a clear understanding of that which is being debunked. The literature on the epistemic implications of CSR shows a wide variety of terms. Some use the term "religious belief."[1] Others use the terms "belief in God" or "belief in gods."[2] Those who use the term "belief in God" appear to have belief in the Christian God in mind. Others are more inclusive and use the term "theistic belief,"[3] or "theism."[4] Theism is often defined as the thesis that there exists at least one god. Therefore, "theistic belief" includes both belief in one god and belief in multiple gods. Still others use the more technical term "belief in a supernatural agent."[5] One author uses "supernaturalistic belief."[6] Some arguments also refer to religious experiences.

My goal is to assess the potential debunking of religious beliefs by CSR theories. As the wide diversity in terms used in the debate shows, some clarifications are called for. Defining what religious beliefs are and setting them apart from nonreligious beliefs is notoriously difficult. Furthermore, religious beliefs are diverse. Some are existential beliefs, like the belief that God exists, while others are more substantial, like "God is love." Many assessments of debunking arguments limit the discussion to just existential beliefs. This does not do justice to the scientific theories. My discussion in the next chapter will make this clear. In this chapter, I will distinguish three groups of beliefs: religious beliefs, existential supernatural beliefs, and substantial supernatural beliefs.

1.2 What Are Religious Beliefs?

Religious beliefs are notoriously hard to define. A lot of definitions have been accused of suffering from a Western or even a colonial bias.[7] Some have also been considered too broad.[8] In later chapters, I argue that the term is used too narrowly to denote belief in the existence of God or gods. Although belief in the existence of gods certainly is a religious belief, the latter is much broader. I discuss the narrower class below under the headers "supernatural belief." Beliefs about how rituals ought to be performed—like how to perform a baptism in Christianity or how to perform an offering in spiritualist traditions—are religious beliefs but not supernatural beliefs. These beliefs might be parasitic on supernatural beliefs,[9] but in themselves they are not. Beliefs about proper religious behavior also fall outside the scope of supernatural beliefs. For example, the Christian belief that one ought to attend church on Sundays is not about the existence or nature of supernatural beings but can be properly called a religious belief.

Like Benson Saler, I will use the term "religious belief" as a family resemblance concept. Use of family resemblance concepts goes back to Ludwig Wittgenstein.[10] It foregoes defining terms in necessary and sufficient conditions and classifies terms by looking at resemblance instead. Saler applies this approach to religion. He advocates that in order to define "religion" we should begin with a small number of uncontroversial examples. Saler calls them "prototypes." For "religion," Christianity or Buddhism could be prototypes. Things can be grouped in the category "religion" when they share a sufficient number of elements with the prototypes. For example, we can see that Islam shares the elements of belief in God and regular worship with Christianity, and therefore Islam can rightly be ranked as a religion. Saler notes that the family resemblance approach leads to vagueness. One borderline case is Confucianism. It shares only a small number of elements with the prototypes, and hence it is not clear whether it can be classified as a religion.[11]

We can apply the same approach to religious beliefs. Some clear prototypes of religious beliefs are as follows:

- The belief that God exists.
- The belief that God revealed himself in Jesus of Nazareth.
- The belief that Gods demand offerings.
- The belief that spirits dwell in forests.
- The belief that a proper offering to Vishnu should use fresh fruits.
- The belief that Christians should attend religious worship at least once a week.

Beliefs can be ranked under "religious beliefs" if they resemble these prototypes to a sufficient extent. Beliefs about the existence of some supernatural being resemble the first prototype. Beliefs about what supernatural beings do resemble the second and fourth. The third, fifth, and sixth prototypes serve to include beliefs about the wishes of supernatural beings and ritual practices.

In this approach there will also be borderline cases. An example is "The universe is a living organism." It resembles, to some extent, belief in the existence of God but is also quite different. Luckily, none of the arguments I discuss in the subsequent chapters refer to such border cases. The family resemblance approach thus suffices for my purposes.

1.3 What Are Existential Supernatural Beliefs?

Some debunking arguments target more specific religious beliefs. They are not too concerned with beliefs about proper ritual practice or historic beliefs about what God did in the past but in beliefs about God or other supernatural beings. Most theories I will discuss in the next chapter also address these more specific beliefs. I will call them "supernatural beliefs" since they are about supernatural beings. As I noted, they come in two varieties. I will first discuss existential supernatural beliefs.

Defining existential supernatural beliefs is far less difficult than defining religious beliefs in general. Supernatural beliefs are a specific subclass of religious beliefs. I define existential supernatural beliefs as

> beliefs that a supernatural being exists.

Existential supernatural beliefs resemble other existential beliefs, like beliefs that human persons exist. Although supernatural beings are considered different from human persons in important ways, beliefs in the existence of both share the idea that there is some being. Existential supernatural beliefs are rather general. Just like an existential belief in human persons does not specify what human persons are like or what they do, existential supernatural beliefs only refer to the mere existence of one or more supernatural beings.

Existential supernatural beliefs can occur as monotheism, the belief that only one God exists, or polytheism, the belief that multiple gods exist. Existential beliefs are, however, not only about God or gods. The vast majority of religious traditions accept the existence of supernatural beings that are not gods. Many Christians believe in the existence of angels; many Muslims in the existence of jinn; and many adherents of animism believe in demons. Belief in the existence of all these beings is ranked among existential supernatural beliefs.

Again, we encounter a problem of vague boundaries. It is not always clear if something is to be regarded as a supernatural being. The pantheistic belief that the universe is a living organism is again such a boundary case.

Though necessary and sufficient conditions for counting something among supernatural beings is again difficult, I propose some sufficient conditions. Naturalists—adherents of the metaphysical view that only natural entities exist and nothing is supernatural—tend to be quick to categorize something as a supernatural being. Most naturalists nowadays are reluctant to limit the natural to the physical, but the nonphysical things they allow for are usually limited to things that supervene[12] on physical things or are at least very common, like social institutions or relations between people. For example, James Ladyman excludes everything that is "spooky."[13] He is not specific about what "spooky" amounts to, but it has an air of being strange or being out of the ordinary about it. In any case, the nonphysical things naturalists allow in their ontology are not beings,[14] so it is safe to say that all nonphysical beings can be counted among the supernatural beings. Some physical beings will, however, also be considered supernatural. For example, members of the Church of Latter-Day Saints hold that God is a physical being. Since the Mormon God resembles the Christian God to a large extent, he can be counted among the supernatural beings.

Naturalists do not usually allow for invisible beings either. The range of invisible beings does not include extinct or long-deceased beings (who cannot currently be seen) but is limited to beings that because of their own nature cannot be seen by humans or have the ability of being unseeable by humans. It is hard to think of such a being that is acceptable for naturalists. Again, not all supernatural beings are invisible in this sense. For example, some Hindu gods, like the avatars of Vishnu, are believed to be visible. So invisibility is also a sufficient but not necessary condition for being a supernatural being.

A final sufficient but not necessary condition is existing outside space and time. No being that exists outside space and time or is able to do so will be acceptable for naturalists. However, many spirits are believed to be bound by space and time just like human beings are or be able to do so.[15]

In summary, I discussed three properties of a supernatural agent that can be considered sufficient conditions. An agent is supernatural if it is

(i) nonphysical;
(ii) invisible; or
(iii) able to exist outside of space and time.

These three sufficient conditions can get us a long way in distinguishing supernatural beings. However, since we lack necessary conditions for what counts as supernatural beings and lack conditions for the broader category of the supernatural, we cannot avoid using the supernatural as a family resemblance concept as well.[16]

1.4 What Are Substantial Supernatural Beliefs?

By substantial supernatural beliefs I mean

> beliefs about the nature of supernatural beings.

Substantial supernatural beliefs move beyond belief in mere existence and specify certain traits of supernatural beings. Some examples are as follows:

- The belief that God is omniscient.
- The belief that God was incarnate in Jesus of Nazareth.
- The belief that spirits demand offerings.
- The belief that gods can be appeased through devotional practices.
- The belief that supernatural beings have special powers.

Some substantial beliefs, like the second and fourth, are specific for a religious tradition, in this case Christianity and Hinduism. The first and third are shared by many religious traditions. The fifth belief is almost universally shared across religious traditions. Some theories I will discuss in the next chapter attempt to explain one or more substantial supernatural beliefs. Some arguments I discuss later target only a limited number of substantial beliefs.

1.5 What Are Religious Experiences?

In this book, I use the term "religious experiences" to denote experiences of something supernatural. In this way the term covers intense mystical experiences of union with the divine and experiences of (vague) supernatural presence. It also covers experiences of possession, where a supernatural being inhabits or takes control of a subject. Though more common in traditions like Voodoo and African Indigenous religions, experiences of possession occur in many cultures. Fabrizio Ferrari describes how devotees of the Indian goddess Sitala "open" themselves by going through preparatory rituals. Once properly prepared, the goddess can enter and take over their minds. When this happens, devotees undergo a trance-like state accompanied by immobility, speechlessness, and goose bumps.[17]

Often the term "religious experience" is used to only refer to intense mystical experiences where a person is overcome by a strong feeling of supernatural presence or enters into a state of union with God. Famous examples are the experiences of Meister Eckhart and Jan Van Ruusbroec. Experiences of this sort are sudden ecstatic interruptions where a subject loses her sense of time and surroundings.[18]

Limiting the argument to mystical experiences greatly limits its scope. Few people have had these intense experiences. For those who did, like Meister Eckhart or Jan van Ruusbroec, it was probably not their basis for their supernatural belief.[19] More people have vaguer experiences that led them to hold supernatural beliefs. Philosopher Basil Mitchel, for example, describes his religious experience as "the sense that I often had, when walking alone in the countryside . . ., that some intense reality was just on the point of breaking through the surface of things and reveaxling itself to me."[20] Another philosopher, Stephen Davis, describes his experiences during a religious service: "I remember the sense that *God* was speaking to me that night. . . . God was somehow picking me out and calling me by name."[21] Kai Kwan gives some examples of religious experiences in his defense of the argument from religious experiences.[22] He gives some examples of people who experienced a vision of Jesus. He also discusses vaguer experiences like "a sublime consciousness of a personalized sustaining power which defies description."[23] Another experience Kwan discusses is "[a feeling of] a presence more personal, more certain, more real than that of any human being, though inaccessible to the senses and the imagination."[24]

During experiences of possession, intense mystical contact with the divine, and vaguer experiences of supernatural presence, people subjectively experience God or another supernatural being. Though all three kinds of experiences are different, the differences are not important for my discussion.

1.6 Conclusion

In this chapter, I distinguished three groups of beliefs: religious beliefs, existential supernatural beliefs, and substantial supernatural beliefs. Both groups of supernatural beliefs are a subclass of religious beliefs. I also discussed what religious experiences are and gave some examples. With the distinctions in mind, we can now look at the science that drives most recent debunking arguments of religious beliefs: cognitive science of religion.

2

CSR: Explaining Religious Belief

2.1 Introduction: Why Cognitive Science of Religion?

My overall goal in this book is to assess whether theories from cognitive science of religion debunk religious belief. Before I provide more background about the theories, I will motivate my choice for CSR. The scientific study of religious belief is vast. Even if we focus on psychological research and omit sociology and history of religions, giving a comprehensive overview of all psychology of religion is not possible. I focus on CSR because, although the discipline is still rather young, it has proven to be the most promising approach for explaining religious belief. Where other approaches offer descriptions rather than explanations, CSR aims to explain why religious beliefs are formed or why religious beliefs are the way they are. CSR theories are also more open to rigorous empirical testing than other approaches. A final reason for my choice of CSR is that it has drawn the most attention of philosophers of religion. Most recent discussion of debunking arguments of religious belief draws on CSR theories.

CSR is a diverse field. It draws on neuroscience, cognitive science, linguistics, and other fields. In this chapter and the next, I will discuss the most prominent CSR theories grouped by their explanandum. A first group explains the evolutionary use of (some) religious beliefs. A second explains how people form religious beliefs by pointing to one or more cognitive biases. A third group explains why people engage in religious rituals. A fourth and final group explains why people have religious experiences.

I cannot provide a complete overview of CSR. The field is still rather young and new theories are being developed every year. I also omitted CSR theories on esotericism[1] and Indian religious practices.[2] These theories only have a limited number of religious phenomena as their explananda. Instead, I limited the discussion to the most discussed and most influential theories in the field that have a broader explanandum. I omitted two widely discussed and influential theories, namely E. Thomas Lawson and Robert McCauley's theory on ritual competence[3] and Tanya Luhrmann's theory of the porous theory of mind.[4] I omitted the first because it does not have many epistemic implications. I omitted the latter because the theory has not been thoroughly developed.

I will discuss twelve theories and briefly discuss their criticisms where available. Most criticisms were raised by other scientists and some are my own. My goal is not to give a verdict on all theories. I merely want to show that the discussion on most theories is far from settled. Christopher Kavanagh, Jonathan Jong, and Aku Visala warn against leaning too heavily on recent cognitive theories of religion when they write, "CSR's theories are still massively underdetermined by data."[5] Their claim might be somewhat overstated,[6] yet some caution is appropriate when arguments lean heavily on these theories. Before discussing each theory in detail, I start with some preliminary observations.

2.2 Adaptationist Theories

A first group of CSR theories explains the adaptive use of religious beliefs. They point to one or more reasons why having religious belief increases the odds of survival or reproduction. Some do note that an adaptive use of religious belief is initially problematic. Scott Atran writes,

> From an evolutionary standpoint, the reasons religion shouldn't exist are patent: religion is materially expensive and unrelentingly

CSR: Explaining Religious Belief

counterfactual and even counterintuitive. Religious practice is costly in terms of material sacrifice (at least one's prayer time), emotional expenditure (inciting fears and hopes), and cognitive effort (maintaining both factual and counterintuitive networks of beliefs).[7]

Despite its apparent maladaptive consequences, some CSR theories do argue that religious belief yields an adaptive use. Two related theories argue that religious belief makes people better at cooperating; one argues that religious belief increases chances at reproducing. All three share the idea that religious belief was transmitted and thrived because of its adaptive use.

2.2.1 Adaptationist Theory 1: The Broad Supernatural Punishment Theory (BSPT)

Two prominent theories claim that supernatural beliefs were (or are)[8] evolutionary advantageous because they helped humans to cooperate. Both stress the moralizing and punishing nature of supernatural beings people believe in. The first one places the rise of supernatural beliefs in biological evolution and the second one in cultural evolution. In this section, I will discuss the first. It is known as the broad supernatural punishment theory (BSPT).[9] The next section will be devoted to the second, known as the big gods theory (BGT). I will mainly rely on Dominic Johnson and Jesse Bering's defense of the theory.

Defenders of the BSPT claim that supernatural beliefs are adaptive. More precisely, they claim that three substantial supernatural beliefs are adaptive:

- Supernatural beings have a moral concern for pro-social human behavior.
- Supernatural beings have privileged epistemic access to human beliefs.
- Supernatural beings punish people who transgress moral norms and reward those who obey them.

I will discuss each of these beliefs and how they are adaptive in more detail.

Supernatural beings have a moral concern for pro-social human behavior.

Defenders of the BSPT claim that supernatural beings are believed to have a firm interest in human moral behavior and more specifically in human pro-social behavior. Pro-social behavior is behavior where humans cooperate with others. People believe that supernatural beings care about how people behave toward each other. Dominic Johnson and Jesse Bering claim that people often believe that rules about how one ought to behave and what one should do stem directly from the expectations or wishes of the gods. The question why the gods have these expectations is rarely asked. The moral relationship with the gods would be similar to an intuitive moral contract, comparable to reciprocal altruism. If humans live according to the gods' expectations and wishes they can expect a reward. If not, they can expect punishment.

According to Johnson and Bering, the alleged expectations and wishes of gods often foster pro-social behavior. Clear examples are norms about fidelity. Many people believe that gods frown upon infidelity. Being faithful to one's spouse was (and is) very important for maintaining trust relations in a community. Being faithful in fulfilling one's obligations is important for cooperation. A faithful person will be less likely to reap the benefits of other people's work without contributing anything herself. Therefore, a divine expectation of fidelity, if obeyed, leads to pro-social behavior.[10] According to Johnson and Bering, the primary locus of supernatural moral concern is the intention of people. An action is deemed bad by gods or other supernatural beings if the person's intentions are bad or good.[11] This brings us to the second adaptive belief.

Supernatural beings have privileged epistemic access to human intentions.

Johnson and Bering confidently claim that "a central component of religious systems are concepts of supernatural agents that have privileged epistemic access to the self's mental states."[12] Having privileged access matters because it implies that people cannot hide their intentions from supernatural beings.[13] Hence, having an intention not to cooperate is enough to deserve punishment. Not all intentions are equally important. Johnson and Bering claim that access to strategic information is most important. Strategic information is information about people's goals and intentions, among which are desires (not) to cooperate and goals (not) to cheat.[14] With access to this information, supernatural beings can reward or punish people even if they merely have the intention not to cooperate.

Supernatural beings punish people who transgress moral norms and reward those who obey them.

According to Johnson and Bering, not only do supernatural beings care about human social behavior, their preferences also lead to punishment or reward in accordance to social behavior. They cite the following evidence: The Ndyuka of Suriname attribute all sorts of misfortunes to sin, ranging from illness and death because of scarcity of food to withholding of divine favors. The Chuuk from Oceania almost always attribute illness to a supernatural cause, as do the Asian Lao Hmong. The Bemba of Zimbabwe believe that relatives who die with a sense of injustice can return and cause harm. Finally, they note that diseases are often associated with violation of taboo. Often the punishment is believed to befall on biological offspring.[15]

Johnson and Bering add that people sometimes go to great efforts to reassert these views (that misfortune is a result of deserved supernatural punishment) when they are confronted with counterevidence. If, for example, they hear about an innocent victim of a crime they tend to see the victim as the instigator of the crime. There also seems to be a general expectation of punishment in the form of negative life events for violations which people committed themselves.[16]

Although both belief in a punishing God and belief in a rewarding God are adaptive, Johnson and Bering add that punishment is more effective.[17] Azim Shariff and Ara Norenzayan provide extra evidence for this last point. They conclude from studies that viewing gods as more punishing and less loving is reliably associated with lower levels of cheating whereas overall belief in gods is not.[18]

Because of these three substantial supernatural beliefs, Johnson and Bering claim that religious belief is overall adaptive. Because of the beliefs, people will be more inclined to obey moral norms. Since these norms are often social this will result in more and better cooperation. Cooperation is very important for human survival, thus more and better cooperation will increase the odds of survival.

Defenders of the BSPT argue that supernatural beliefs are particularly helpful in avoiding free riding behavior. Free riders are people who reap the benefits of cooperation without paying any of the costs. Free riders pose a danger to evolutionary fitness for three reasons. First, they take advantage of other people's energy and thereby reduce the other's fitness. Second, when people know free riding is prevalent they could refrain from cooperation and diminish their own chances of survival and reproductive success. Third, trying to find out whether someone is a free rider or someone trustworthy demands time and effort, which could be used in a more evolutionarily advantageous way. Ruling out free riders or reducing their prevalence is thus undeniably evolutionary advantageous.

It can be doubted whether the BSPT needs all three supernatural beliefs. It is not clear why privileged epistemic access is necessary. Cooperation is an action. It seems that belief in gods who have a moral concern and who will punish or reward people in accordance with their actions can be equally adaptive. Here people will still have a strong incentive to do the right actions (i.e., cooperate). They might have the wrong intention for doing so, but having a wrong intention will not result in less cooperation and thus in lower evolutionary fitness. Johnson and Bering would likely respond that supernatural beliefs will "work better" if intention is taken on board. For example, behavior will be more convincing or more determined with the right intention. Johnson and Bering also argue that intention is sometimes required to distinguish between pro-social from antisocial behavior. They give the example of a man who holds a door open for a woman. The man might have the intention of reducing uncertainty of who proceeds first or he might have the intention of reinforcing gender stereotypes. In both cases the action is the same, yet in the first his action is considered pro-social and in the second antisocial. The only way to differentiate between them is by looking at the man's intentions.[19] I do not see how this provides compelling evidence for the claim that intentions matter from an evolutionary point of view. In both cases the behavior will be the same and thus equally (mal)adaptive.

2.2.1.1 Criticism

Broad supernatural punishment has been criticized on multiple grounds. Luther Martin and Donald Wiebe doubt whether many people really believe in morally concerned gods. They draw support from the Hebrew Bible to show that supernatural belief often led to antisocial behavior like tribal conflicts and wars.[20] They claim that supernatural beliefs only supported pro-sociality for historically contingent reasons (Martin and Wiebe 2014). Defenders of broad supernatural punishment could claim that pro-sociality and cooperation are not opposed to war and tribal conflict. Conflict and war require a great deal of cooperation and pro-sociality toward one's own group. Supernatural belief could make it easier for people to organize an army to combat their enemies. In doing so, they increase the chances of survival for themselves and their offspring. Martin and Wiebe's criticism is thus not obviously valid.

Amber DeBono, Azim Shariff, Sarah Poole, and Mark Raven provided evidence against the efficacy of supernatural belief by showing that priming subjects with "forgiving god" concepts made them more prone to steal.[21] They thereby provide evidence that at least some supernatural beliefs foster antisocial behavior.

Others assumed the pro-social moral concern of supernatural beings but doubt the efficacy of supernatural beliefs for pro-social behavior. Ryan McKay and Harvey Whitehouse argue that there is no straightforward connection between supernatural belief and more pro-social behavior. They claim that the close connection stems largely from a prejudice among scientists and that unclear notions of "religion" and "morality" have blurred research. One of these prejudices is that the Western conception of "religion" is more in line with Abrahamic religions than other (Eastern) religions. They add that the concept of "religion" is often not precise enough. The concept of "morality" is regularly taken to be a "family friendly" conception of morality (and pro-sociality), according to McKay and Whitehouse. The question whether religion (or supernatural beliefs) is related to pro-sociality is thus sometimes cashed out as the question whether belief in gods makes people "nice." McKay and Whitehouse argue that pro-sociality cannot be equated to "being nice" straightforwardly.[22] Azim Shariff nuances the effect of supernatural beliefs when he writes, "Does religion increase moral behavior? Yes. Even though the effect is parochial, bounded, transient, situationally constrained, and often overstated, it is real."[23] Some have responded and claimed that the criticisms are exaggerated.[24]

These last criticisms are harder to reconcile with the theory than the criticisms by Martin and Wiebe. They cast doubt on whether supernatural belief could really aid humans in cooperating.

2.2.2 Adaptationist Theory 2: The Big Gods Theory (BGT)

A second, related adaptationist theory is the Big Gods Theory (BGT). The theory bears great resemblance to the BSPT but differs by putting the adaptive use of supernatural beliefs in cultural evolution. Whereas supernatural beliefs were not adaptive for most of human evolution, belief in moralizing, punishing supernatural beings grew to be adaptive at a later stage. Groups with these beliefs outcompeted groups with other supernatural beliefs because they allowed humans to live in larger groups. This implies that some people held (or still hold) beliefs in supernatural beings that are not moralizing, punishing, and/or all seeing.

Defenders of the BGT take "moralizing" to encompass both a moral concern for pro-social behavior and a punishment or reward in accordance with moral rules. Therefore, the BGT's portrayal of supernatural beliefs is similar to that of the BSPT's. Defenders of the BGT will often write about gods being omniscient rather than epistemically privileged, but this makes little difference for the theory. Defenders of the BGT do not stress the importance of human intention and supernatural access to it.[25] I noted above that this need not make much of a difference since the BSPT probably can do without this belief as well.

Contrary to defenders of broad supernatural punishment, defenders of the BGT do not claim that the three adaptive supernatural beliefs (privileged epistemic access, moral concern, and willingness to reward or punish, in short, belief in big gods) appear cross-culturally. Supernatural beliefs of this kind only rose to prominence when people started living in large groups. For a large part of their history people had no real need for supernatural monitoring to have them obey pro-social norms. Human groups were sufficiently small to be monitored by kin or other closely related individuals. Reciprocal altruism and kin selection also allowed for enough cohesion to have smooth cooperation. None of these, however, permits large-scale cooperation. Belief in big gods does permit this.[26] By living in large-scale communities, groups with moralizing gods became more successful and outcompeted other groups.

Shariff et al. give three reasons why their theory is preferable to the BSPT. The first is that the BSPT cannot explain large-scale cooperation. Secondly, they claim that there are less costly routes how natural selection can address the problem of cooperation. Lastly, they claim that the historical and archaeological evidence favors the BGT over the BSPT.[27] The first reason seems to demand too much of the BSPT since it never set out to explain large-scale cooperation. The second reason is hard to verify. Therefore, I focus on the third reason, namely that the archaeological and empirical evidence favors the BGT. The evidence they cite for disagreeing with the BSPT is historical and archaeological. Shariff at al. claim that many gods are whimsical when it comes to morality. In most small-scale societies people also do not believe that gods are omniscient. Gods of smaller societies often cannot observe people outside of village boundaries.[28] Shariff et al. also refer to a study by Frans Roes and Michel Raymond. Their survey of societies showed that large-scale societies are more often characterized by belief in moralizing gods.[29]

According to Norenzayan, supernatural beliefs function in the same way as belief that one is being watched. Norenzayan supports his claim with experiments he conducted with Will Gervais and refers to similar experiments conducted by others. A first experiment suggested that being primed with god concepts had similar effects as being primed with concepts involving social surveillance by people, since both led to an increase in self-awareness. Jared Piazza, Jesse Bering, and Gordon Ingram found a similar effect. They instructed one group of children not to look in a box and then left the room. A second group of children was told the same thing with the remark that an invisible supernatural agent called Princess Alice was in the room. The second group showed less cheating than the first.[30] A second experiment suggested that implicit God primes (participants had ten sets of five words that contained God concept) have the same effect. Two more experiments with a comparable setup also reported that implicitly priming god concepts reduced cheating.[31] In the last experiment, participants tended to give more socially desirable responses, both when primed by god concepts and by social surveillance concepts.[32]

Norenzayan also draws support from reports of the so-called "Sunday effect." Unlike the experiments above, these reports have the benefit of not being set in an artificial environment and therefore provide real-life evidence for BGT.[33] Deepak Malhotta conducted a field study on how willing people are to respond to online appeals for charity. On Sundays, appeals to Christians were three times more effective than on other days.[34] Benjamin Edelman compared internet porn consumer rates in highly religious communities to consumer rates in less religious communities. The comparison showed that the average rates did not differ much but within highly religious communities the rates went down on Sundays.[35] According to Norenzayan, the "Sunday effect" is due to higher exposure to religious primes on Sundays.[36]

Norenzayan makes the caveat that all the evidence is correlational and does not allow strong claims about causation.[37] Making claims about causation requires manipulation; in our case making claims about when supernatural beliefs have a causal effect requires a manipulation of supernatural beliefs. Manipulating religiosity is very difficult, if not impossible, so establishing a causal relation will be too.

2.2.2.1 Criticism

Much of the criticism on broad supernatural punishment also applies to the BGT. Apart from these, some have also criticized the theory on other grounds. Pascal Boyer and Nicholas Baumard argue that a lot of large-scale societies did not believe in big gods. Especially the gods of the Roman Empire and early kingdoms in the Near East appear to be undisturbed by a moral conscience and uninterested in human morality. They seemed more concerned with receiving sacrifices in due time and obedience.[38] Boyer and Baumard thus argue that historical data does not match the picture the BGT sketches. Some defenders of the BGT respond that Roman gods did have some moral concern. For example, Romans used their gods to back up oaths. To be adaptive, belief in supernatural beings must above all make people contribute their fair share. Whether gods have a moral conscience themselves is less important. However, many gods of large-scale societies seem to lack even this minimal moral concern. The gods of ancient mystery religions often encouraged isolation from society and thus antisocial behavior. More historical research on the presence and prevalence of the role of religious belief in encouraging pro-sociality could settle this debate.

Harvey Whitehouse et al. collected historical evidence showing that large-scale societies emerged *before* belief in big gods and argue that belief in big gods therefore cannot enable large-scale cooperation. They argue that belief in big gods could still have played a role in maintaining or reinforcing large-scale cooperation.[39] While their criticism does speak against a central tenet of the BGT (namely that belief in big gods enabled large-scale cooperation) it does not exclude that belief in big gods was selected for by cultural evolution. Defenders of the BGT responded that Whitehouse et al. did not properly classify societies as lacking belief in big gods. They argue that more research is needed to assess when societies developed belief in big gods and if it preceded large-scale cooperation.[40]

Defenses of broad supernatural punishment can also be considered criticisms of the BGT. If belief in morally concerned, punishing gods with privileged epistemic access is indeed a biological adaptation (as defenders of broad supernatural punishment argue) groups with big gods did not outcompete other supernatural beliefs with the rise of large-scale societies (as defenders of the BGT argue). Here again historical and anthropological research can show if belief in moralizing supernatural beings is or was also widespread in small-scale societies.

2.2.3   Adaptationist Theory 3: The Attraction of Religion Theory (ART)

The most recent adaptationist theory connects supernatural beliefs to sexual selection. As yet, no widely shared name has emerged for this theory. I will call the theory the attraction of religion theory (ART), in line with the title of the recent book *The Attraction of Religion*[41] in which research on the theory is brought together.

The ART is rooted in sexual selection theory. Jason Slone and James van Slyke define it thus:

> Sexual selection theory argues that a number of traits and behaviors we see in sexually reproducing species evolved because they help to facilitate not survival per se but rather reproductive success by either making the individual attractive to the opposite sex or by deterring same-sex rivals.[42]

Sexual selection theory thus argues that some traits and behaviors increase the odds that an individual will be able to pass along his or her genetic material. Some traits and behaviors signal information that has an attractive force. Examples of such information are being strong or being wealthy. The most effective signals are costly and useless[43] because they are hard to fake and thereby reliable indicators of an individual's fitness.[44]

Defenders of the ART claim that some religious traits or behavior can signal information that has attractive force. Slone and Van Slyke summarize the ART's central thesis as:

> Religion is widespread because it is attractive to people, and it is attractive to people because it helps to manage the suite of adaptive problems related to reproduction via the costly signaling of strategic information useful for attracting, acquiring, and retaining mates, ensuring paternity certainty, preventing mate defection and infidelity, encouraging parental investment, and more.[45]

One example of information that can be signaled through religious behavior is fidelity. Bulbulia et al. note that infidelity can lead to resource loss for both men and women. The loss is, however, greater for men because female infidelity can lead to men investing their resources in offspring that does not carry their genetic material. Women do not face this problem since they give birth to their own offspring. Bulbulia et al. claim that prayer can signal fidelity. To argue for this point they refer to the BGT (see above). The BGT predicts that belief in God is associated with pro-normative behavior and restraint from acting out of self-interest. They also refer to McCullough and Willoughby, who found belief in God associated with greater self-regulation and inhibition.[46] Michael McCullough and Brian Willoughby conclude from a survey of studies that there is strong evidence for a robust association between religion and self-control and religion and conscientiousness. They also find substantial evidence that children of religious parents tend to have more self-control. They do acknowledge that the evidence for a causal link from religion to self-control is meager. Furthermore, the evidence for the claim that religiousness promotes self-monitoring is mixed. Some of their results support this, but other studies found no such relationship. McCullough and Willoughby also found no evidence for the claim that religion in itself fosters the development of self-regulatory strength. Some religious rituals, like prayer, do seem to support self-regulation.[47]

Another piece of information that can be signaled is the ability to draw resources from other (unrelated) exchange partners. This is important because bringing up children requires help from outsiders. People with higher social prestige are usually more successful in getting help from others. This piece of information can be signaled by church attendance. Bulbulia et al. cite a study by John Shaver who noted that church attendance was associated with greater social standing and reputation in Fiji.[48] John Shaver and Sosis found that men's ascribed rank significantly predicted their frequency of church attendance in Fiji.[49] Bulbulia et al. note from their own study that church attendance in New Zealand occurs among groups with mainly unrelated individuals,[50] which is evidence for the claim that religion broadens one's social network. Matthew Martinez and Pierre Lienard argue that especially rites of initiation might benefit social standing and hence increase reproductive fitness.[51]

2.2.3.1 Criticism

Craig Palmer and Ryan Begley criticize the ART because it cannot explain many religious rituals and is contradicted by some religious behavior. They note that many religious acts cannot plausibly lead to reproductive benefits. Clear examples are lifelong asceticism and lifelong celibacy. One could respond that these are exceptional, but Palmer and Begley respond that ascetics and celibate monks are usually seen as exemplars and inspire many religious people to follow them. The ART also leads to predictions that are not met according to Palmer and Begley. An obvious prediction drawn from the ART is that selfish behavior should increase when individuals near the end of their reproductive years to make sure previous abstinence is balanced out. This prediction is not met.[52]

2.3 Cognitive Bias Explanations

In subsequent sections of this chapter I will discuss a number of theories that explain supernatural beliefs by pointing to a cognitive bias or mechanism. Though some of these theories also refer to biological evolution, the key difference from the previous group of theories is that they refer to the operations of one or more cognitive mechanisms to explain religious phenomena. The theories I discuss below are the preparatory account, the hyperactive agency detection device, the moral dyad, the existential theory of mind, and the cognitive optimum. For these theories, fewer criticisms were formulated. Before discussing the theories, I start with some preliminary remarks.

2.3.1 Preliminary 1: Cognitive Mechanism

The theories I will discuss and evaluate all share the idea that supernatural beliefs are produced by a cognitive mechanism. The term "cognitive mechanism" is used rather loosely. Related terms are "cognitive module," "cognitive pattern," or "psychological mechanism."

All cognitive theories I will discuss share a commitment to a number of claims:

(i) Cognitive mechanisms are not mere transmitters of input but have an active role in shaping the content of the beliefs they produce.
(ii) There is no distinct cognitive mechanism that produces religious beliefs but religious beliefs are produced by a cognitive mechanism that is also responsible for other beliefs.
(iii) The cognitive mechanism that produces religious beliefs is overly active or overreaching when producing supernatural beliefs.
(iv) Cognitive mechanisms produce intuitive religious beliefs.

Claim (i) is fairly uncontroversial in modern cognitive science. Cognitive scientists have largely abandoned the idea that the external world determines belief and that the human apparatus merely transmits what is given by external reality.[53] Some authors cash out this idea in terms of the mind being governed by theories. For example, some have discussed the theory-ladenness of perception.[54] Another well-known example is the idea that social cognition is guided by an implicit, unarticulated theory of mind.[55] Beliefs are thus the way they are not solely because of the input they receive but also because of the parts, operations, and organization of the cognitive mechanism that produce them. Virtually all theories in CSR subscribe to claim (i).[56]

Claim (ii) is also almost universally made by CSR theorists.[57] They argue that there is no designated religious cognitive mechanism. Religious beliefs are instead produced by cognitive mechanisms that also, and mainly, produce other beliefs like beliefs about agents, other people or morality. This claim is connected to the "naturalness thesis," which is also (almost) universally accepted by CSR theorists.[58] In its bare essentials the thesis states that religious beliefs are nothing special or exotic but are a normal result of human cognitive makeup.

Claim (iii) builds on claim (ii). The theories I will discuss below all suggest that supernatural beliefs result from some kind of overactivation of a cognitive mechanism. When not in a state of overactivation, the mechanism produces other, nonreligious beliefs. Some authors I will discuss below are explicit; others are less clear but still their theories can be interpreted in this way.

Claim (iv) is also commonly assumed by CSR theorists and is cause of some confusion.[59] It states that the cognitive mechanisms that CSR theorists discuss produce (above all) intuitive beliefs. An influential paradigm in cognitive science distinguishes two systems involved in the formation of beliefs and two corresponding kinds of beliefs.[60] An early defender of this view is Dan Sperber. He proposes to distinguish intuitive from reflective beliefs. Sperber defines "intuitive" as follows: "In order to hold them as beliefs, we need not reflect—or even be capable of reflecting—on the way we arrived at them or the specific justification we may have for holding them."[61] Intuitive beliefs are usually beliefs that are formed spontaneously, for example, by perception. Beliefs that are formed through unconscious inferential processes that take intuitive beliefs as their premises also count as intuitive beliefs according to Sperber. An example is the belief that sparrows are birds. It requires an inferential process that ranks sparrows among the birds because they are similar enough to an exemplar. This process usually remains unconscious.[62]

Reflective beliefs lack the immediacy of intuitive beliefs. According to Sperber, they are to be distinguished from intuitive beliefs because they are embedded in a "validating context." Sperber's examples of validating contexts are "reference to authority, to divine revelation, explicit argument or proof, etc."[63] According to Sperber, the most common way in which we acquire reflective beliefs is through communication. Sperber claims that reflective beliefs are the result of a more conscious process.

Another author who discusses what distinguishes "reflective beliefs" from "intuitive beliefs" and their relation is Justin Barrett. According to Justin Barrett, intuitive beliefs[64] can influence reflective beliefs in three ways. First, intuitive beliefs serve as default options for reflective beliefs. For example, when a girl is seen taking an apple from the kitchen every day, most people will form the intuitive belief that the girl does this to satisfy her own desires. This can subsequently serve as input to form the reflective belief that the girl is hungry. Upon getting new information—for example, that the girl is seen feeding the apples to a horse in order to gain the horse's confidence—the intuitive belief can be overridden and the reflective belief revised. Without extra information the reflective belief supported by the intuitive belief will seem more likely.[65] Secondly, intuitive beliefs make some reflective beliefs more plausible than others. Reflective beliefs that fit with or do not violate intuitive beliefs seem more plausible. Third, intuitive beliefs shape experiences that we use as evidence to form reflective beliefs.[66]

All CSR theories I discuss below (tacitly) assume the distinction between intuitive and reflective beliefs. They point to various cognitive mechanisms that produce intuitive supernatural beliefs. These intuitive beliefs can in turn give rise to reflective supernatural beliefs. Most theorists are not explicit on what happens to intuitive beliefs before they become reflective. Some see a role for culture or implicit instruction. Many cognitive scientists rightly acknowledge that probing intuitive beliefs is hard. While some probe them by doing experiments on young children, others do so by looking for cross-cultural similarities.

The focus on intuitive beliefs by the theories I discuss below has an important implication for the role they can play in the arguments I discuss in the next chapters. Since they are often vague about what happens to an intuitive belief before it becomes a reflective one, they are in an important way limited as an explanation of reflective religious beliefs.

2.3.2 Preliminary 2: Universal Cognitive Mechanisms?

All theories I discuss below claim or suggest that the cognitive mechanism that produces (intuitive) supernatural beliefs is universally shared by all normally functioning humans. Since the cognitive mechanisms produce intuitive supernatural beliefs, which shape reflective supernatural beliefs, defenders of CSR theorists tend to argue that supernatural beliefs are rather similar. Pascal Boyer writes,

> The explanation for religious beliefs and behaviours is to be found in the way all human minds work. I really mean *all* human minds, not just the minds of religious people or some of them. I am talking about *human* minds because what matters here are properties of minds that are found in all members of our species with normal brains.[67]

Boyer, like other CSR theorists, acknowledges that supernatural beliefs are diverse but argues that the diversity does not go very deep. He claims that people will not form just any supernatural belief but that the cognitive architecture partly determines what supernatural beliefs are acceptable. For example, the belief "There is only one God! He is omnipotent. But he exists only on Wednesdays" will not sound very believable to most humans. A belief like "There is one God! He knows everything we do" will most likely sound much more believable. Boyer claims that similarities are not found on the surface level but require a look at a deeper level.[68] He continues by making the following analogy:

> Suppose you were a Martian anthropologist and observed that all human beings sustain themselves by eating food. You could compare the different tastes of food the world over and try and find common

features.... It would seem [to the Martian anthropologist] that there are many, many different foods on earth and no simple way of finding the common elements. But now imagine you were a *good* Martian anthropologist. You would study the chemistry of cooking, which would reveal that there are only a few ways to process food... and a large but limited number of ingredients.[69]

Boyer thus argues that supernatural beliefs show a great deal of similarities. Since most CSR theories focus on intuitive beliefs and state that these intuitive beliefs are the product of the operations of a shared cognitive mechanism, the similarities are best looked for at this level. How far the similarities go on the reflective level remains an open question that most CSR theorists do not address.[70]

2.3.3 Preliminary 3: Cognitive Biases as a By-Product

Cognitive bias theories are different than the adaptationist theories I discussed earlier in this chapter. Whereas the adaptationist theories try to explain supernatural belief by pointing to its adaptive value, cognitive mechanisms take a different route. According to all the theories I will discuss in this section, supernatural belief has no adaptive value itself.[71] They argue that supernatural belief emerged as a by-product of a mechanism that was itself adaptive.

2.3.4 Cognitive Theory 1: The Preparatory Account (PA)

A first cognitive bias theory is the preparatory account (PA).[72] The theory argues that humans are biased toward forming some beliefs that prepare the way for religious beliefs. The PA explains religious beliefs by referring to a number of biases. They are the teleological bias, the dualist bias, and a bias toward afterlife beliefs. These biases (be it individually or separately) result in religious beliefs or make religious beliefs easy to acquire.

The first and most documented bias is the teleological bias. Deborah Kelemen and her team conducted most of the studies on this bias. She observed that young children have a tendency to reason about natural things in terms of purposes and that children easily suppose that natural things are intentionally created.[73] In one experiment, four- and five-year-old American children usually answered the question "what is this for?" in teleological terms. They answered that lions are here for visiting in the zoo and clouds for making it rain.[74] The bias is still present in seven- or eight-years-olds. When American seven- or eight-years-olds were asked questions like "why is a rock pointy?" they gave answers like "so that animals wouldn't sit on them and smash them" or "so that animals could scratch on them when they got itchy."[75] Kelemen found that the bias begins to lose its strength around the age of nine.[76] Margaret Evans also found evidence for a bias in children to endorse intentional accounts of how species originate.[77]

Unlike children, adults prefer causal mechanistic explanations to teleological ones. Causal explanations would suppress the teleological bias when adults learn scientific explanations. This was confirmed by a study on Romani adults. The study followed a similar methodology as the studies mentioned above. The experiment showed that Romani adults with little or no scientific training were more likely to give teleological explanations than adults with scientific training. Kelemen theorizes that the teleological bias recedes when children learn about mechanistic explanations; it does not, however, disappear completely. A study with undergraduate students, who had learned causal explanations for natural phenomena, showed that teleological explanations were explicitly judged as correct significantly more when the subjects were under time pressure.[78] Krista Casler and Kelemen conclude from this that the teleological bias is not a childhood phenomenon that inevitably gets revised and replaced through maturation but a cognitive default that may exist throughout life.[79]

The teleological bias thus makes people prone to see teleology or design in the world. While the bias is more prevalent in young children, the research cited above makes it plausible that it remains operative in adulthood under certain conditions like time constraints.

A second bias that could prepare the way for supernatural beliefs is a dualist bias. This bias leads us to think that bodies and souls are distinct entities.[80] According to Paul Bloom, mind-body dualism is a natural by-product of the fact that we have two distinct cognitive systems, of which one deals with material entities and the other with social entities. Bloom claims that most people think of the mind as identical to the soul.[81] The bias makes it possible to think of souls without bodies. Since gods are often thought to possess soul-like qualities but also as not having a body, the dualist bias could prepare the way for supernatural beliefs.

Marjaana Lindeman, Annika Svedholm-Häkkinen, and Jari Lipsanen argue that a similar, though broader, bias is important to explain religious beliefs. According to them, the dualist bias should be expanded to "core ontological confusions." They claim that humans have "core knowledge." They define "core knowledge" as "a narrow but fundamental set of ontological knowledge about evolutionarily important psychological, biological, and physical phenomena."[82] Examples are knowledge that mental phenomena are different than physical phenomena, animate beings are different than inanimate objects and living organisms are different than lifeless objects.[83]

Clearly "core knowledge" consists of a set of beliefs about the ontological structure of the world. It resembles the idea of "folk physics."[84] Lindeman et al. claim that religious and paranormal believers do not honor the distinctions that follow from the ontological structure. For example, many religious believers believe that the mind has an independent existence just like physical objects and many paranormal believers believe that material objects can be controlled by the mind by means of psychokinesis or that thoughts can heal a person. The "core ontological confusions" thus occur when "the distinctive properties of the superordinate categories of mental and physical, animate and inanimate, and living and lifeless are inappropriately mixed."[85]

It is not clear whether Lindeman et al. maintain that the "core knowledge" is subject to cultural variation. Boyer argues that "folk physics" are part of the general human architecture and hence to a large extent universal. When Lindeman et al. claim that core knowledge is usually learned without instruction at a young age, they suggest that it can be subject to cultural variation. In this regard, their examples of core ontological confusions (confusion between the mental and physical domain, confusion between animate and inanimate objects) are Western examples of core ontological confusions. Cultures where people believe in ontologies without a distinction between the mental and the physical or without inanimate objects can be expected to have different core ontological confusions.

A third bias is a tendency toward forming afterlife beliefs. Jesse Bering and David Bjorklund conducted three experiments that suggest a bias toward afterlife beliefs in young children. In three experiments, children were shown a puppet show featuring an alligator and a mouse. During the puppet show, the children learn that the mouse is feeling sick, sleepy, hungry, and thirsty. At the end of the show the alligator eats the mouse. Afterward, the children were asked whether the mouse was dead. Most children answered "yes." Then the children were asked ten more questions. Some addressed whether the mouse's biological functions still worked (e.g., "does his brain still work?"). Others asked whether it would still feel sick, sleepy, hungry, or thirsty. The older group of children was significantly more likely to answer that biological functions did not continue, but the younger group also showed a relatively firm understanding that biological functions ceased after death. The younger group did show a much stronger tendency than the older group to answer that the mouse's psychological states (being sick, sleepy, hungry, or thirsty) continued after death. The middle and adult group in the third experiment were significantly less likely to report that biological or psychobiological states continued. Bering and Bjorklund claim that their findings lend support to the hypothesis that afterlife beliefs decrease over time. They attribute the decline to increased biological knowledge.[86]

Various authors have offered explanations for these findings. Bering himself argues that afterlife beliefs result from what he calls "simulation constraints." Whereas the absence of one's own physical, bodily states is fairly easy to imagine or simulate,[87] absence of one's own mental states is not. Failure to think of oneself in a state without mental states results in the belief that these states continue.[88] Mitch Hodge, Sousa, and White note that Bering's account does not explain why people cross-culturally hold afterlife beliefs but no pre-life beliefs. If Bering were right, people would also not be able to simulate a state before they had mental states and would form pre-life beliefs. Yet most people do not have pre-life beliefs.[89] Shaun Nichols argues that people have difficulties imagining the proposition "it is the future and I do not exist."[90] Judith Bek and Suzanne Lock reject the idea that afterlife beliefs result from some simulation constraint because before one can simulate what it is like to be death one has to be convinced that surviving biological death is possible. Their alternative is that afterlife beliefs arise because deceased people are still categorized as persons and the category "person" is intuitively associated with having mental states even after biological death.[91] Hodge argues for something similar.[92] Lane at al. suggest that afterlife beliefs arise because children do not have a good idea of what biological death means.[93] Mitch Hodge, Sousa, and White suggest that afterlife beliefs might be a means of managing the fear of death; the idea that humans will die would cause paralyzing terror and afterlife beliefs are a means of coping with it.[94]

The third bias thus makes people prone to believe that humans can and usually do survive biological death. While some functions may be believed to cease (especially biological functions), those that make up personal identity[95] continue.

The PA can be construed in two ways: one of the three biases can prepare the way for supernatural beliefs or a combination of two or three biases can. Any combination of biases can prepare the way for religious belief. Belief in teleology can easily lead to belief that some supernatural being is responsible for that teleology. Belief in dualism can lead to belief in immaterial beings, which we saw is a form of supernatural belief (see Section 1.4 in Chapter 1). Subjects who believe in an afterlife believe that there is more to reality than the world we perceive. This belief likely makes religious beliefs easy to acquire.

2.3.5 Cognitive Theory 2: The Hyperactive Agency Detection Device (HADD)

The theory of the hyperactive agency detection device (HADD) is arguably the best-known CSR theory. Its main defender is Justin Barrett, who was inspired by Stewart Guthrie's theory of animism and anthropomorphism. I will first discuss Guthrie's theory and then continue with Barrett's.

Guthrie summarizes his theory as follows:

> Central here is my account of anthropomorphism and animism, as residual, retrospective categories of perceptual and conceptual mistakes. They consist in thinking that we have detected human or other animal agency, or one or more of their characteristics, when in fact we have not. They arise inevitably, as by-products—namely, as false positives—of our scanning an uncertain world for what matters most. What matters most is agency, especially complex agency, and prototypically that of our fellow humans. We are unconsciously geared to detect such agents by varied perceptual sensitivities and . . . we have a low threshold for judging that we have detected them.[96]

Guthrie states that supernatural beliefs emerge as a result of mistakes in agency detection. He argues that the human ability to detect agents is easily triggered to produce the belief that agents are around on very limited evidence. This leads humans to conclude that there is an agency behind things where no agent is involved. Guthrie argues that these "false agents" later become supernatural agents.

Justin Barrett agrees with Guthrie that people have a strong bias to interpret ambiguous evidence as caused by an agent.[97] A bias toward agency makes sense from an evolutionary point of view. Barrett writes, "If you bet that something is an agent and it isn't, not much is lost. But if you bet that something is not an agent and it turns out to be one, you could be lunch."[98] Barrett notes that the HADD is especially likely to be triggered when objects seem to be moving in a goal-directed manner. Often the input HADD draws on are patterns known to be caused by agents.[99]

Barrett is clear that not all outputs of the HADD are supernatural beliefs. He also does not go as far as Guthrie in claiming that the HADD can fully explain religious belief. He does claim that the tendency to attach agency to objects contributes significantly to the formation of religious concepts.[100] According to Barrett, this is most obvious in identifying ambiguous things, like "wispy forms"[101] as ghosts or spirits. When input like wispy forms is fed to our agency detection mechanism, the outcome is likely to be belief in a ghost or spirit. Without sufficient reflective defenses,[102] this nonreflective belief will become a reflective one. Barrett adds that this will happen "whether the sighting is an illusion or not."[103] It is not clear what Barrett means when he writes "whether the sighting is an illusion or not." It suggests that beliefs about ghosts or spirits can be formed by both actual ghosts and spirits or by things that resemble them but, in fact, are something different.

Barrett claims that our hyperactive tendency to find agency can contribute to supernatural beliefs in a second way. It can foster the belief that "known agents are exhibiting agency."[104] Here Barrett's account resembles Kelemen's findings (see Section 2.3.4). By identifying input as caused by agency, the HADD could reinforce the supernatural beliefs a subject already has. For example, registering a cloud as an agent that acts purposefully could reinforce the belief that a certain god controls the weather. In these cases, no new belief is formed, but an existing belief in superhuman agents is reinforced.[105]

In Barrett's theory, detection of agency by the HADD is not the end of the matter. After the HADD is triggered, the theory of mind (ToM) begins to reason how and why the detected agent acted. The ToM is usually put to use to form beliefs about other people. For example, by means of the ToM, a subject can form the belief that someone is angry when the subject sees a frowny face. When some input is identified as caused by an agent, ToM makes similar inferences about that alleged agent. The subject could hereby forms beliefs about what detected invisible agents are like or what they want to do.

In the end, Barrett is rather skeptical whether the HADD can fully explain how people form religious beliefs. He notes that religious beliefs require a lot of cultural input as well. Barrett's example is a man (Lupe) who forms beliefs about the existence of "the Chivo man," a part-goat, part-man creature. Initially, Lupe's HADD produce beliefs in an unseen agent but he dismisses it reflectively. At a later time, Lupe hears stories about "the Chivo man" living in the neighborhood and she subsequently comes to believe in its existence.[106] Barrett's worries can be avoided when focusing on vaguer supernatural beliefs, like the belief that something supernatural exists. In Barrett's theory, the working of the HADD and the ToM could suffice to produce beliefs of this sort.

2.3.6 Cognitive Theory 3: The Moral Dyad Theory (MDT)

Kurt Gray and Daniel Wegner defend a theory known as the "moral dyad." They argue that moral thinking takes a dyadic form, which has supernatural belief as a by-product. When people find themselves in moral situations, they would always look for a moral agent—the one who does the moral action—and a moral patient—the one who receives it. Gray and Wegner argue that all moral acts are (at least implicitly) parsed in this dyadic way.[107] According to Gray and Wegner, agency can be tied to moral agents and experience to moral patients. They define both as: "Experience is the general capacity for sensation and feelings and includes the capacities for hunger, fear, pain and pleasure. Agency, in contrast, is the capacity to do and intend, and includes the capacities for self-control, judgment, communication, and memory."[108] They claim that agency is necessary to be a moral agent whereas experience is necessary to be a moral patient.[109] Because of the connection of moral agents to agency and moral patients to experience, children and animals are considered solely as moral patients since they lack agency. On the opposite side, God is solely seen as a moral agent because most people believe that he cannot be harmed by actions of others.[110]

There are situations where the dyad appears to be incomplete. An example is a situation where someone has sex with a dead chicken and then eats it. There appears to be no moral patient in this case. In cases like these, people will infer to the presence of a victimized patient; for example, this could be the memory of the chicken or children whose morals might be twisted when they learn about what happened. Gray and Wegner acknowledge that examples can be found that explicitly deny that there is any victim, but the automatic reflex to look for a victim will always be there. Similarly, cases without apparent moral agents will automatically prompt people to seek one. For example, someone who trips on a sidewalk will sometimes sue the homeowner and someone who chokes on a hamburger might sue the cook.

In many cases, isolated patients will infer to God as the moral agent.[111] In a study participants were asked to make judgments about the mental qualities of a fetus, an infant, a five-year-old girl, an adult woman, an adult man, a respondent, a man in a persistent vegetative state, a frog, a dog, a chimpanzee, a dead woman, God, and a robot. The participants were also asked to rank them along the two dimensions: "moral experience" and "moral agency." Moral patiency includes the abilities to feel hunger, fear, pain, pleasure, rage, and desire; the idea that people have personality and consciousness; and the ability to feel pride, embarrassment, and joy. Moral agency includes the abilities to have self-control, morality, memory, emotion recognition, planning, communication, and thought. Normal adult humans were judged high in both "experience" and "agency." Infants and animals scored high on "experience" but low on "agency." The fetus and the persistent vegetative state man were judged to have low "experience" and no "agency." The dead woman was judged to have none of either. Finally, both the robot and God were judged high on "agency" but low on "experience."[112] This indicates that God is mainly thought of as a moral agent and not as a moral patient. Especially in events like natural disasters people would infer to God because no human is powerful enough to bring about such a thing.[113]

Gray and Wegner add that there can be other reasons to believe in God as well, like providing meaning to a potentially meaningless life or providing order in a chaotic world but claim that the main reason why people see God acting in the world is to explain otherwise inexplicable salvation and suffering. They add that cases of isolated suffering are probably more powerful than positive events.[114] Statistics from the United States provide evidence for their claim. The states with the highest suffering are also the states with the highest level of religiosity.[115]

2.3.7 Cognitive Theory 4: The Existential Theory of Mind (EToM)

Jesse Bering defends a theory, known as the existential theory of the mind (EToM). He argues that supernatural beliefs result from overactivation of the ToM. The ToM—the human ability to reason about other people's minds and intentions—would have expanded into other domains than social cognition like religion. Bering argues that the operations of the ToM make individuals perceive some psychological agency (God) as having encoded communicative intentions in life events, just like the ToM sometimes makes individuals perceive human psychological agency in symbolic deistic gestures.[116] Bering's examples of how people perceive human psychological agency in deistic gestures are as follows: "A threatening glance from a stranger, a gentle tug of a child's hand on one's sleeve, and the rolled eyes of a disgruntled student."[117] These actions are more than mere gestures; they communicate something about the person's mental states.

According to Bering, the human ToM draws conclusions about mental states not only from human behavior but also from events in nature or events in life. These events are experienced as meaningful in a similar way to the deistic gestures mentioned above. A meaningful event implies purpose or intention. Therefore, meaningful events are interpreted as communications from some psychological agency. Because meaningful events do not fit into any category of known behavior from agents (like humans or animals), humans infer to an agent of another ontological category. The agent is seen as having orchestrated the meaningful event out of its own will and having framed the event as a symbolic device to give a message to the experiencing subject.[118] In short, a supernatural being is believed to communicate with people by investing meaning in natural or life events.[119]

According to Bering, a person needs to attribute mental states to the agent(s) in order to interpret meaning.[120] Therefore, the supernatural being will be believed to have a mind or to be able to have mental states. Concluding to a supernatural being does not require explicit causal reasoning; it rather comes naturally. All that is required for the EToM to produce supernatural beliefs is that humans have built up an understanding of intentional relations. It does not require further (cultural) external sources.[121]

Bering's theory differs from Justin Barrett's HADD because the EToM infers to an agent causing meaning and not to agency itself. Bering illustrates the difference with an example. On the HADD, a girl who witnesses a tumbling rock can attribute mental states to the rock itself. On Bering's own EToM, she will rather infer that some supernatural agent caused the rock to tumble to deliver a message. In the second case, she perceives not so much agency as she perceives the intention behind the event.[122]

Bering suggests an evolutionary account of why the EToM evolved. The EToM would have evolved as a by-product because human evolution invested a lot in the theory of mind. He writes, "So much has human evolution invested in the Theory of Mind system, that the drive to attribute mental states has expanded into corridors of human cognition that probably had nothing whatever to do with the system's initial selection."[123]

2.3.8 Cognitive Theory 6: The Cognitive Optimum Theory (COT)

Arguably the most influential CSR theory is Pascal Boyer's cognitive optimum theory. Other than the bias theories I discussed above, his theory does not explain how religious beliefs are formed in individuals but mainly explains how supernatural beliefs are transmitted and why they matter to people. He argues that minimally counterintuitive concepts have the best chances of being remembered and being transmitted. People would have intuitive ontological categories like "plant," "animal," or "person." These categories allow for predictions. For example, categorizing something under "plant" allows the inference that the thing will not be able to move and will grow under the right conditions.

Minimally counterintuitive concepts violate some of the expectations that come with their intuitive ontological category. For example, a ghost is usually categorized under "person" but violates the expectation that persons cannot move through walls. At the same time, the majority of expectations is retained and a ghost is expected to perceive things in the same way as persons do and to interact with others as persons do. Minimally counterintuitive concepts differ from intuitive (concepts that violate no expectations) and maximally counterintuitive concepts (concepts that violate many expectations). Intuitive concepts, like "John Doe," are not memorable because they are ordinary. Maximally intuitive concepts, like a man who is 30-meter long, has 11.5 arms and only appears every second Tuesday of the month, require too much cognitive effort to remember. Most supernatural concepts are minimally counterintuitive and thus easily (optimally) transmitted and remembered.[124]

At first glance, Boyer's theory attempts to explain how people form supernatural beliefs. He offers a mechanism that explains why people tend to believe in minimally counterintuitive concepts of which supernatural beings are the most eye-catching examples. After a closer look, however, his theory explains rather why some supernatural beliefs are believed rather than others. Boyer writes:

> The many forms of religion we know are not the outcome of a historical *diversification* but of a constant *reduction*. The religious concepts we observe are relatively successful ones selected among many other variants. . . . [T]he many variants that our minds constantly produce and the many fewer variants that can be actually transmitted to other people and become stable in a human group. . . . People's minds are constantly busy reconstructing, distorting, changing and developing the information communicated by others. This process naturally creates all sorts of variants of religious concepts, as it creates variants

of all other concepts. But then not all of these variants have the same fate. Most of them are not entertained by the mind for more than an instant. A small number have more staying power but are not easily formulated or communicated to others. An even smaller number of variants remain in memory, are communicated to other people, but then these people do not recall them very well. An extremely small number remain in memory, are communicated to other people, are recalled by these people and communicated to others in a way that more or less preserves the original concepts. These are the ones we can observe in human cultures.[125]

Boyer's theory thus does not explain why supernatural beliefs occur but why the human mind prefers some supernatural beliefs to others. After laying out his mechanism, Boyer does address the question of why people believe in supernatural beings.[126] He discusses Guthrie's and Barrett's theories but finds them wanting. He then formulates a version of the BSPT.[127] This makes clear that Boyer also believes he needs another explanation for why supernatural beliefs occur (widely) on top of his COT.

2.4 Conclusion

In this chapter I discussed eight theories from CSR that explain religious belief. I distinguished two groups of theories: adaptationist theories that point to the adaptive use of religious beliefs and cognitive bias theories that point to one or more biases to explain why people form religious beliefs. In the next chapter, I discuss two other groups of CSR theories, theories that explain ritual behavior and theories that explain religious experiences.

3

CSR: Explaining Ritual Behavior and Religious Experiences

3.1 Introduction

Whereas most CSR theories explain religious beliefs, some explain other religious phenomena. Two widely discussed phenomena are religious rituals and religious experiences. I defined "religious experience" in Chapter 1. I take religious rituals to be

> actions aimed at engaging with or pleading with supernatural beings.

Many religious rituals are merely aimed at engaging with supernatural beings.[1] These actions are not aimed at anything more than feeling divine presence. Examples are the Christian Eucharist or Eastern devotional practices.

Other religious rituals are aimed at getting effects in daily affairs or inter-personal relations. These actions are not aimed at drawing closer to God or other supernatural beings but aim to move supernatural beings to help or change things in the world. Examples are petitionary prayer or offerings.

3.2 Theories Explaining Why People Take Part in Religious Rituals

Below I will discuss two theories that aim to explain why people partake in religious rituals. Although the theories can refer to one or more beliefs, they mainly aim to explain behavior. Defenders of both theories do not explicitly discuss how accompanying beliefs about why and how rituals should be performed are formed. I will assume that those beliefs arise along with ritual behavior

3.2.1 Ritual Theory 1: The Costly Signaling Theory (CST)

A first theory explaining why people take part in religious rituals is the costly signaling theory (CST). Defenders of the theory argue that people take part in religious rituals because doing so signals honesty or reliability. The idea of costly signaling has been debated among evolutionary biologists for some time and was first applied to religion by Laurence Ianneconne.[2] The most elaborate defenses have been offered by Richard Sosis.[3] Others have defended similar views.[4] Like the BSPT and the BGT, the CST argues that religion benefits cooperation, but in a different way.

The theory draws on a well-known mechanism in evolutionary biology, namely, signaling behavior in animals. The textbook examples of costly signaling in the animal kingdom are the stotting behavior of springboks and the peacock's tail. Springboks will sometimes jump into the air with all four feet off the ground simultaneously. This act does not aid in escaping from predators and even slows the springbok down or tires it out. One prominent explanation of stotting behavior is that springboks signal how fit and strong they are and thereby let predators know that they are not worth pursuing. Since most springboks that engage in stotting are male, it is also possible that stotting behavior signals show off strength to potential female mating partners. While at first glance maladaptive (stotting behavior makes springboks vulnerable and thus reduces their odds of surviving and reproducing), the signals sent by engaging in stotting behavior can be adaptive in the long run by scaring off predators and attracting more females. A similar explanation is offered for the peacock's tail. The tail makes it very visible for predators but also displays an excess of resources.

Like other CSR theories, costly signaling holds that religion is the key to solving the problem of free riders. They would also aid human cooperation in general. *How* religion does this is rather different on this theory. By engaging in rituals people show that they believe in one or more supernatural beings and they show their allegiance to the social norms the supernatural beings dictate. Richard Sosis adds that in order for honest signaling to work, the displays must be costly and hard to fake.[5] When an individual shows her commitment in this way, she will likely be more successful in survival and reproduction, because more people will be willing to cooperate with her.

Sosis provides empirical data to back up the CST. The theory predicts that religious communities have better cooperation and thus a longer longevity because religious communities (with costly rituals) tend to have more trust and better cooperation. His analysis of nineteenth-century collectivist communities shows that religious communities outlasted secular counterparts four times on average. Furthermore, the most successful communities posed the strictest religious entrance demands and thus required more costly displays.[6] Other evidence comes from studies showing that people are more likely to donate to fellow ritual participants than to others. A study by Sosis and Ruffle among Israelis in religious and secular settings found that ritual participation among religious Israelis strongly predicted stronger generosity to fellow religious Israelis when compared to the generosity of secular Israelis.[7] A team led by Dimitris Xygalates concludes from experiments that extreme rituals have a deeper effect than less extreme rituals on pro-sociality. They examined two Hindu rituals in Mauritius that involved body piercing with multiple needles, carrying heavy structures, and dragging carts attached by hooks to the skin. Both participants and observers were asked to engage in a donation task. The results were then compared to a similar donation task with participants in and observers from a less intense ritual, namely collective prayer. The researchers reported that participants in and observers of extreme rituals made significantly higher donations.[8]

3.2.1.1 *Criticism*

Michael J. Murray and Lyn Moore heavily criticize the CST. They claim that rituals as a marker of honesty are unstable as an evolutionary trait because signaling will be equally beneficial when the signaler is dishonest.⁹ Bulbulia and Sosis respond that costly rituals are "hard to fake," meaning that one cannot easily produce the signal without an underlying commitment to a supernatural being and its norms.¹⁰ Murray and Moore react that in the majority of religious rituals, the costs are fairly minor compared to the advantages gained. Engaging in practices like refraining from eating pork or praying daily is not at all hard to fake compared to the benefits gained.¹¹ Defenders of the CST can respond that extreme rituals *are* hard to fake and that extreme rituals result in higher evolutionary benefits than the low-cost rituals to which Murray and Moore refer. Xygalates's studies on extreme Hindu rituals suggest so. Extreme rituals of this sort are, however, rather rare and therefore CST has problems in explaining the wide prevalence of people who only engage in low-cost rituals.

Murray and Moore provide an additional reason to doubt that extreme rituals are evolutionary stable. With extreme rituals the costs are very high and the individual drastically reduces her fitness. The evolutionary benefits are rather low by comparison and it is often unclear what the benefits will be. Engaging in extreme rituals does not make it plausible that a person will be regarded as honest and therefore does not guarantee greater odds of survival and reproducing. Therefore, performing extreme rituals is not an evolutionary stable strategy, according to Murray and Moore.¹²

Another problem is that engaging in rituals, however costly they may be, does not always signal a commitment to pro-social norms dictated by a supernatural being. A Hindu who engages in worship or a Buddhist who engages in meditation signals a commitment to the goals of self-fulfillment rather than to some social norm. Furthermore, Eastern and some Western religious practices often have the effect of people *renouncing* social norms. In the East, religious practices often result in an ascetic lifestyle, with little interest in society or normal everyday life. In the West, there are also ample examples of religious practices where people withdraw from society, for example, in ascetic monasteries. Rituals of this sort disrupt cooperation rather than fostering it. A world-renouncing, ascetic way of life could even promote free riding because social norms, especially norms about collaborating, are considered less important.

3.2.2 Identity Fusion (IF)

The identity fusion theory (IF) explains how religious rituals can forge communities or create strong groups. Harvey Whitehouse argues that (religious) rituals have an important role in shaping societies. Rituals, and especially intense, less frequent rituals, are said to fuse personal identities together and create closely knit communities.[13]

According to the IF, (religious) rituals can serve as "social glue" that binds communities together. Whitehouse distinguishes two kinds of social glue, "social identification" and "identity fusion," of which the latter is the strongest.[14] He argues that people are able to formulate personal self-concepts and social self-concepts, which they use to classify themselves and others into groups. The classification is quite strict so there are clear boundaries between where personal self-concepts end and where social self-concepts begin.

Whitehouse claims that rituals are important for social identification. Rituals leading to social identification are usually high frequency, low arousal rituals. Examples are Sunday mass for Catholics or Friday prayer for Muslims. People engage in these rituals once a week and the experiences during them are usually not very intense. Whitehouse argues that because these rituals are practiced frequently it is impossible for participants to recall the details of every single occasion. As a result, they come to represent the rituals and their meaning as types of behavior; Catholics will represent Sunday mass as Holy Communion and Muslims Friday prayer as the Call to Prayer. Ritual types of behavior are accompanied by "procedural scripts" and "semantic schemas"; the former specifies what generally happens during a ritual and the latter what is generally believed to be its significance. The existence of procedural scripts and semantic schemas allows the tradition to be generalized beyond people of immediate acquaintance and allows people to identify with everyone who performs similar acts and holds similar beliefs. According to Whitehouse, this routinization of rituals is a necessary condition for the emergence of "imagined communities."[15] Imagined communities are defined as "large populations sharing a common tradition and capable of behaving as a coalition in interactions with non-members, despite the fact that no individual in the community could possibly know all the others, or even hope to meet all of them in the course of a lifetime."[16] Besides instilling conformity, routinization of rituals also makes learning and transmission of complex doctrines and narratives easier.

The second, much stronger, kind of social glue is "identity fusion." Whitehouse defines "identity fusion" as "a visceral sense of oneness with others in one's group." For fused individuals the boundary between what is personal and what is social becomes porous. Triggers of one's sense of personal self also serve as triggers of the social self. As a result, threats against one group member can prompt the same defensive reactions as a personal attack.[17] In contrast to social identification, the boundaries between personal self-concepts and social self-concepts are far less clear and even seem to disappear. According to Whitehouse, identity fusion is widespread in kin groups and other small social units where members share the rituals and tribulations of life. This happens because fusion of identities occurs when individuals experience "high arousal" events together. Clear examples of high arousal events are times of hardship, for example, a family that experiences a traumatic event during a war.[18]

Though it often emerges as a result of events over which people have no control, identity fusion can also be cultivated by rituals. The rituals are more intense and less frequent. Examples are rites of initiation. According to Whitehouse, intense rituals are somewhat like traumatic events but can be even more powerfully bonding experiences. The main reason is that rituals are "causally opaque," meaning that they can be interpreted in a wide variety of ways. A traumatic event prompts a rather limited array of questions, like "who was to blame?" or "why did this happen to me?" In rituals there is a lot more room for speculation and the range of interpretations is more open-ended. Because of this the significance of rituals is more likely to increase over time, whereas the significance of traumatic events is likely to decay. When people engage in rituals in a communal setting they observe others undergoing the same experience and can imagine that they share the same rich interpretative process. By sharing personal experiences with a special group of others, rituals can cause group members to fuse.[19]

Whitehouse suggests that identity fusion can also be cultivated by especially compelling narratives. His example is the narrative of Jesus of Nazareth's death on the cross. His death on the cross can be very convincingly equated with people's own suffering to such an extent that it may be possible to fuse with Jesus's identity. When many people fuse with a person from a narrative, it will lead to a fusion between these people as well.[20]

The importance of rituals in social identification and identity fusion is not limited to religious rituals. Whitehouse considers the highly ritualized and highly emotional gatherings of the Nazi Party at Nurnberg as occasions for identity fusion.[21] He also conducted a survey among Libyan revolutionaries during the conflict in Libya in 2011. Revolutionaries who had fought on the frontline reported levels of identity fusion with other fighters comparable to the fusion they felt with family members. Fighting on the frontline thus almost literally created "brothers in arms."[22] An experiment conducted by Emma Cohen, Roger Mundry, and Sebastian Kirschner confirmed that secular rituals can also lead to greater social cohesion but also suggests that religious rituals are more successful in this regard. They set up an experiment with two groups performing the same drumming ceremony. One group was primed with religious concepts and the other with secular concepts. The group primed with religious concepts showed a trend toward higher cooperation.[23]

3.2.3 The Hazard Precaution Theory

The hazard precaution model was defended by Pascal Boyer and Pierre Liénard.[24] The theory aims to explain ritual actions, like blessing with water or kneeling that make up a larger ritual. They acknowledge that rituals are more than the mere sum of ritualized actions. They claim that ritual actions are characterized by their stereotypy, rigidity, repetition, and apparent lack of rational motivation. They argue that ritual behavior, and its stereotypical aspects, can be explained by the operations of two cognitive systems, the hazard precaution system (HPC) and action parsing (AP). The HPC's role is the detection and reaction to perceived threats. AP directs the division of flow of behavior into meaningful units. In some cases, interaction between both systems creates ritual behavior.

According to Boyer and Liénard, rituals share five characteristics:

(1) *Compulsion*. Under certain circumstances, people feel that it would be dangerous, unsafe or, improper *not* to perform ritual actions. Anxiety would prompt an emotional drive to perform the action. Performing the ritual action provides some relief.
(2) *Rigidity*. People usually feel that some ritual action should be performed in the precise way that it was performed earlier. They attach negative emotions to deviations or changes and sometimes consider doing so dangerous.
(3) *Goal-demotion*. Performing of individual ritual actions is divorced from observable goals. Boyer and Liénard do acknowledge that the overall ritual script often has a goal, but argue that it is often not clear what the subgoal of individual ritual actions like kneeling or blessing is.
(4) *Internal repetition and redundancy*. The same action is performed repeatedly. Often ritual actions need to be performed an exact number of times.
(5) *A restricted range of themes*. Many ritual actions appear to focus around themes like pollution, purification, danger, and protection. Ritual spaces are described as pure and safe. The point of many rituals is to purify or cleanse participants.[25]

The joint operations of the HPC and AP can explain these common features. Perceived threats or danger would trigger the HPC. The HPC responds by making subjects perform certain actions. These actions are subsequently parsed by the AP and parsed as part of one larger ritual. They way humans respond to perceived threat by the operations of the HPC and how they parse the actions that result from it can explain the common features (1–5).

Because they perceive danger, subjects feel *compelled* (1) to respond. Because the HPC is triggered by perceived threat, its responses (the ritual actions) focus on themes related to threat like pollution, purification, etc. (5).[26] The response of the HPC is undeliberate or automatic. Humans have intuitions about what actions are appropriate responses to the perceived threat, which would stem from evolutionary history. The intuitions, however, are usually not consciously accessible. The reactions of the HPC can also easily overload a subject's cognitive system to the effect that she loses sight of what she is doing or why she is doing it. This explains why ritual actions appear not to be aimed at a specific goal (3) and are nonetheless performed with rigidity (2). The AP classifies the actions produced by the HPC in one category and as part of a larger sequence. When a set of ritualized actions is parsed as constituting one overall action, goals can be assigned to that overall action. In this way ritual scripts can be aimed at a goal, although subjects are unaware of the goals of each individual ritualized action that make up the script.

The ritual actions that the HPC triggers resemble how patients who suffer from obsessive compulsive disorder (OCD) often act. Like OCD patients do on a regular basis, people would fail to appreciate the real level of danger and to respond to it in an appropriate way. This would lead in failure to realize when an action has been completed. This, in turn, leads to repetition (4).

By overloading the cognitive system, ritual behavior has a soothing effect and reduces anxiety. Ritualized actions, however, only provide temporary relief. This leads to an interesting feedback loop according to Boyer and Liénard. Perceived threat triggers the HPC and AP to perform ritualized actions but the feeling of perceived threat soon returns. Ritualized action, in turn, strengthens the feeling of perceived threat by making it more salient. As a result, the HPC and AP respond with more ritualized actions.[27]

Boyer and Liénardcontinue that rituals recruit the HPC and AP. Many cognitive systems other that HPC or AP are recruited in other domains than the domain it evolved for. For example, frogs evolved an automatic response to snap at any small objects that comes within its visual field. The system, however, evolved to only snap edible objects like flies. A cognitive system is recruited in other domains when the input in the new domain resembles the input of the original domain. According to Boyer and Liénard, participants in rituals are fed input that triggers the HPC and AP. Participants (or rather initiates) are told that a ritual *should* be performed and are thereby led to conclude that not performing the ritual is dangerous. For example, rituals are said to prevent war, to lead to a successful harvest or to cure the sick. Sometimes rituals are claimed to be performed to ward off evil. This all raises awareness of threat.[28]

3.3 Theories of Religious Experiences

A final group of theories explains why people have religious experiences. Like I did in the first chapter, I focus on religious experiences where subjects putatively experience God or another supernatural being. I will first discuss neuroscientific study of religious experiences, followed by Michael Persinger's theory, and then the predictive coding theory.

3.3.1 Neural Correlates of Religious Experiences

Two famous studies looked at the neural correlates of religious experiences during prayer and during meditation. Mario Beauregard and Vincent Paquette looked at the brain activity of fifteen Carmelite nuns while they were subjectively in a state of union with God. The nuns were asked to remember the most intense mystical experience they ever had. During interviews conducted after the experiment, several nuns mentioned that they had felt the presence of God, his love, and plenitude and peace. The researchers found significant activation in the right medial orbitofrontal cortex, right middle temporal cortex, right inferior and superior parietal lobules, right caudate, left medial prefrontal cortex, left anterior cingulate cortex, left inferior parietal lobule, left insula, left caudate, and left brainstem. Beauregard and Vincent regard the complexity of brain activity as evidence that mystical experiences are complex and multidimensional. They involve changes in perception, cognition, and emotion. The brain areas where significant activity was measured are used in other experiences of perception, cognition, and emotion as well. Beauregard and Paquette do acknowledge that the study was limited because participants were asked to remember mystical experiences rather than trying to have an actual mystical experience.[29]

A team of neuroscientists led by Nina Azari probed the neural correlates of experiences during religious recitation. They asked six evangelical Christians and six non-Christians to recite a psalm while under a PET scanner. The resulting PET images showed higher activation in the right dorsolateral prefrontal cortex in the religious subjects than in the nonreligious subjects. The religious subjects also showed lower activation in the dorsomedial frontal cortex and the right precuneus. These areas are used during cognitive processes. This indicates that the experiences were more emotional than cognitive for religious subjects. The researchers claims that their findings support the view that religious experiences are an attributional phenomenon, meaning that religious experiences are not simply constituted by the experienced input but by causal claims where an experience is attributed to a religious source.[30]

3.3.2 Michael Persinger's God Helmet

Michael Persinger and his team went one step further and tried to artificially induce religious experiences where subjects feel a (supernatural) presence.[31] Before trying to create these experiences,

Persinger had speculated that experiences of a sensed presence could be the result of changes on the temporal lobe caused by changes in magnetic fields. Magnetic stimulation would cause small, transient, electrical micro-seizures within the deep structures of the temporal lobe. The temporal lobes are linked with the subjective sense of the self. Persinger notes that deep brain structures, like those in the temporal lobe, are known to respond to stimulation by not representing the concurrent sensory input. In this case, the temporal lobes would not represent the input of the actual self but produce a distorted sense of the self, that is, a sense of an external invisible self. Persinger argues that the temporal lobes could be more receptible for micro-seizures after life crises, drug use, or energy deprivation.[32] Persinger conducted experiments where subjects' temporal lobes were stimulated by magnetic forces from a helmet (the "god helmet"). In line with Persinger's prediction, the subjects reported experiences of a sensed presence.[33] Though a replication of the experiment failed, Persinger and his team stand by their initial results.[34]

3.3.3 Predictive Coding

Predictive coding is an influential theory in neuroscience and cognitive science. It aims to explain how human perception and action works. Recently, predictive coding has been applied to religious experiences. I will give a general introduction to predictive coding first and then discuss its application to religious experiences.[35]

3.3.3.1 *Predictive Coding*

Predictive Coding (PC) is a theory that is gaining traction in neuroscience and cognitive science.[36] The main idea is that the brain is a Bayesian prediction machine which constantly runs and updates mental models of the environment. By operating in this way, the human mind can maximize accuracy and efficiency. The operations of the "prediction machine" heavily shape perception. The mind shapes perception by constantly predicting what the subject will perceive.

The core of PC is adequately captured by Hawkins and Blakeslee when they write, "Your predictions not only precede sensations, they determine sensation."[37] During perceptual experiences, the brain would run a model of the world and makes predictions about the causes of sensory input. For example, when a subject walks through a forest, her internal model will predict visual perceptions caused by trees. The model will shape perceptual experiences in such a way that incoming rays of light are processed as trees. The brain can do so because the model it runs has information about the statistical structure of some set of observed input. In other words, the model predicts what objects (or persons) the subject is likely to experience. In this way, the brain is always guessing what will happen next. The expectations will influence what perceptual experiences the subject will have.

The human brain is, however, not blind to the external world. While the model usually tries to match all sensory input to the existing model of the world,[38] the brain also looks for sensory input that does not match its model of the world. When this occurs, the brain makes "prediction errors." When prediction errors occur, there is a mismatch between the prediction of the model and the sensory input. Prediction errors prompt the brain to update its internal model of the world.

An important epistemological question is why PC can be expected to be a reliable guide to the world. Karl Friston argues that PC works toward an optimal model by regulating free energy. Updates of the internal model of the world are governed by what he calls "the free energy principle."[39] The principle states that the brain will work toward minimizing free energy or surprise in perceptual experiences. Since prediction errors lead to friction between the model and the world, it leads to more surprise than a smooth fit. Therefore, the brain will be less prone to surprise if it updates its model of the world to prevent prediction errors. Although Friston does not state this explicitly, he suggests that the free energy principle also prevents PC from updating the model too much. Pausing at every sensory input to see whether it matches the internal model in detail will hamper efficiency. Therefore,

PC seeks a balance between accuracy and speed in the internal model. Over time, the balance will nonetheless tip in favor of accuracy.

3.3.3.2 Predicting Religious Experiences

Recently, PC has been applied to religious cognition. The theory received its most elaborate defense by Marc Andersen. He draws on two older approaches to religious cognition, the HADD and Persinger's ideas on religious experiences. I discussed both earlier in this chapter. Although Andersen regards both approaches to religious cognition as flawed, he suggests that some insights can be incorporated in a new theory in line with PC. He argues that people will be more prone to overdetect agents (see HADD) or feel a sensed presence (see Persinger) when their internal model of the world expects more invisible agents or persons around. He thereby accepts that humans can be hyperactive in their agency detection and that suggestion can lead to feelings of a sensed presence. When a subject believes that invisible agents exist, the belief will act as a top-down filter on how her sensory input is experienced. She will thus be more prone to identify noises or patterns as caused by an invisible agent. Raising suggestions, by making a subject aware that someone or something could be around can also increase the likelihood that input will be identified as supernatural.

Andersen argues that agency detection and experiences of a sensed presence are to a large extent the result of the context in which the subject finds herself. The context comes with certain expectations about what the subject could experience. The context in which a subject perceives and experiences is to some extent determined by her cognitive makeup[40] but is to a large extent the result of social and cultural factors. Social and cultural factors can foster what Andersen calls "priors about supernatural agents." One possible source of priors about supernatural agents are religious teachings and texts. Another source is guided processing of ambiguous stimuli. An example is how some Pentecostal Christians are taught to interpret certain bodily sensations as signs from God. Some Pentecostal Christians learn to identify a tingling feeling in their stomachs as caused by the Holy Spirit.[41] The PC framework suggests that once a bodily sensation is identified with a cause (like God), prior beliefs will grow stronger. Andersen also notes that in many religious traditions believers are encouraged to engage in several forms of sensory deprivation. For example, Muslims and Christians are required to fast and some Hindus are encouraged to perform extreme rituals.[42] Andersen argues that these practices force the brain to rely more on priors than under normal circumstances because the brain has less energy to spend.

Andersen also argues that the nature of many religious concepts makes it hard to filter them out of the internal model of the world. Many gods and spirits are believed to be invisible or even imperceptible. Concepts of gods and spirits are also flexible and evasive. Because of these features, religious concepts are impervious to error revision.[43] Andersen seems to suggest that religious priors do not lead to clear, testable predictions. A subject who believes that spirits exist will expect that spirits will cause rustling of leaves or patterns in nature. She will not expect that *all* or even *most* rustling of leaves and patterns are caused by spirits. When she discovers that she erroneously regarded some ambiguous input as caused by spirits, she will be less prone to revise her model.

Michiel van Elk and André Aleman apply the PC approach to a number of religious phenomena.[44] They argue that religious hallucinations or visions are likely related to imprecise coding of predictive signals. They also argue that mystical experiences, where the subject feels a loss of ego or identity can be explained by changes in multisensory integration. Multisensory integration is the process whereby information from multiple modalities (sense, touch, vision, etc.) is brought together to form a coherent image of the body and the environment. Due to some changes, integration could go wrong and result in mystical experiences. They also argue that PC can explain why people pray or sense a supernatural presence. Here expectations that govern social interactions are applied to invisible beings.

3.4 Conclusion

In this chapter I discussed five theories from CSR. I two theories that explain why people engage in religious rituals; and five theories that explain why people have religious experiences.

4

Are CSR and Religious Belief Incompatible?

4.1 Introduction

In this chapter I critically evaluate a number of arguments for the conclusion that CSR theories are incompatible with three substantial supernatural beliefs. If one of the arguments is valid and if the CSR theory on which it relies is true, one or more substantial supernatural beliefs can no longer be regarded as true.

The arguments I discuss below target the following beliefs:

- Religious beliefs are caused by God.
- Religious beliefs result from revelation.
- People can engage with God by partaking in religious rituals.

Before I discuss each of the arguments in detail it is worth noting that none of the arguments targets the existential belief that God exists. The truth and epistemic status of this belief is still the most hotly debated issue in analytic philosophy of religion. While CSR theories do weigh in on this debate (see Chapter 5), they do not do so by means of an incompatibility argument.

The beliefs that are targeted are two metabeliefs about religious beliefs and one religious belief about the function of religious rituals. If the two metabeliefs are rendered unjustified by one of the arguments below, the costs for religious believers are not very high. A religious believer can hold on to supernatural beliefs that are central to most religious traditions, for example, that God exists or that God is such and such. A successful argument against the third belief has more severe consequences. Religious believers in most traditions have high esteem for their rituals. In many cases, this is likely because they are regarded as a means of engaging God or another supernatural being. If the argument is successful, believers should look differently to their rituals.

4.2 What Is the Incompatibility Argument?

To my knowledge, no author defended a fully fleshed-out argument for incompatibility between CSR theories and religious belief.[1] Some pop-science books do hint at an incompatibility argument but they remain rather sketchy. Jesse Bering writes that religious belief evolved as an "adaptive illusion."[2] Dawkins refers to a number of CSR theories before stating that religious belief results from an in-built irrationality mechanism.[3] It is not immediately clear what Dawkins's argument is but he suggests that the picture CSR theories sketch is incompatible with the truth of religious belief. Some YouTube videos and blog posts also suggest that the incompatibility between CSR theories and the truth of religious belief is obvious, although they do not specify how or what religious belief they target.[4] Daniel Dennett is somewhat more precise. He surveys the theory of HADD and the COT and claims that they amount to a "fiction-generating contraption"[5] or a "fantasy-generation process."[6] They would make the brain "churn out hypotheses" of which some stick around. Dennett suggests that science shows that religion has little to do with what religious believers claim it does. He makes no argument to substantiate this claim.

Some defenders of religious belief accuse CSR theorists of suggesting incompatibility claims. They cite work by prominent CSR theorists and highlight phrases that suggest incompatibility. Justin Barrett finds such suggestions in the work of Paul Bloom. Barrett notes how Bloom presents the scientific evidence as showing that natural systems *go awry*[7] and infer desires and goals *where none exist*.[8] Bloom does not explicitly state that religious belief is illusory and false, but it is hard to interpret his remarks in a different way according to Barrett. David Leech and Aku Visala cite a number of passages where other CSR theorists hint at incompatibility. They note that Scott Atran[9] sometimes suggests that the counterintuitiveness of religious ideas (see Chapter 2 Section 2.3.8) boils down to counterfactuality.[10] They also claim that Atran's use of the term "quasi propositions" betrays a negative view of religious beliefs. Atran writes, "Religious quasi propositions may have *truth value* (e.g., Baptists believe that 'after you die you either go to Heaven or Hell'), but they are *not truth-valuable* in the sense of being liable to verification, falsification, or logical evaluation of the information."[11] Leech and Visala also accuse Pascal Boyer of making incompatibility claims. Boyer writes, "The question is . . . why . . . some concepts of *imagined* entities and agents rather than others matter to people?"[12] Elsewhere he writes, "Religious notions are products of the supernatural *imagination.*"[13] It is not clear, though, whether Atran and Boyer started out with the assumption that supernatural beings are illusory or whether they drew their conclusions from CSR theories.

Others made more elaborate arguments. These authors aim to preempt possible challenges to the epistemic status of religious belief or merely aim to show that there was never any incompatibility. Jonathan Jong, for example, writes, "*Prima facie*, naturalistic explanations and theological explanations of phenomena in general appear to be in mutually exclusive competition."[14] David Leech and Aku Visala write, "Critics of religion have recently claimed that the natural explanation of religious-belief formation offered by the Cognitive Science of Religion . . . is incompatible with theism."[15]

4.3 The Argument Stated

We saw how a lot of authors make suggestions for how an incompatibility argument could go (some more elaborate than others), but none makes a precise statement. Most also do not specify the religious belief that is (allegedly) incompatible with CSR and why this is the case. In this section I will construe a well-developed argument on the basis of these implicit suggestions.

First of all it is important to note that in themselves CSR theories and religious belief cannot be incompatible or stand in mutual competition. Both can, and do, coexist. The emergence of one need not result in the eclipse of the other.[16] There is no clear incompatibility because CSR theories and religious belief are two very different things. As all beliefs, religious belief is a doxastic state people can be in. CSR theories provide a description of the mechanisms that produce religious belief, of the evolutionary pressures that gave religious belief its edge, of why people engage in religious rituals or why people have religious experiences (see Chapter 2 & 3). Because they are very different things, it is hard to see how religious belief and CSR theories can stand in mutual opposition.

The incompatibility could be more indirect. If CSR theories would imply that religious beliefs are false, it is clear that the two are incompatible. A well-known example of a scientific theory that implies the falsity of a substantial supernatural belief is the theory of evolution. Some religious believers believe that God created the earth in six days' time less than 10,000 years ago. If the Darwinian theory of evolution is true, it implies (among many other things) that the earth is much older and emerged gradually over millions of years.

What the authors above probably are getting at when they raise the issue of incompatibility is that CSR theories also imply that some substantial supernatural or religious belief is false. They thereby suggest that there is a possible conflict between the propositional content of claims made in CSR theories and some propositions that religious believers, as religious believers, believe. As most theories do, CSR theories make certain claims about what is true. In this case, claims are made about the evolutionary history of religious belief and/or about the cognitive systems that give rise to it. Religious believers hold some propositions (like "God exists" or "people's souls go to heaven after biological death") to be true as well (however, see the discussion of premise 2 below). An incompatibility argument states that some CSR claims and some religious claims stand in mutual incompatibility.

The incompatibility argument can be stated as follows:

(1) CSR theories state true propositions.
(2) Religious believers, as religious believers, hold that some propositions are true.
(3) Some of the propositions stated by CSR theories conflict with propositions which religious believers, as religious believers, hold to be true.
(4) Two (or more) conflicting propositions cannot both be true.
(5) Therefore, some propositions held to be true by religious believers, as religious believers, are not true.[17]

All five premises of the argument can be questioned, though some will be doubted more than others. Premise 1 will be questioned by some philosophers of science.[18] A majority of them probably agree that scientific explanations do state true propositions or aim to do so, but some argue that scientific explanations are aimed at empirical adequacy rather than truth.[19] When it comes to CSR theories, most theorists in the field appear to aim at true propositions. Some theories make claims about the evolutionary use of rituals or religious beliefs and thus about why they were selected for by natural selection. Other explanations make claims about which mechanisms produce religious beliefs and/or about the proximate causes of religious belief. Assessing whether CSR theories are aimed at truth or something else (let alone assessing whether scientific theories in general are aimed at truth or not) lies far beyond the scope of this chapter. I will therefore proceed as if CSR theories are aimed at stating true propositions.

Apart from debates about whether scientific theories are aimed at truth or not there is another reason to doubt premise 1. We noted in Chapter 2 that some doubts can be raised about the status of CSR theories.[20] For this reason premise 1 is also not uncontroversial among CSR theorists themselves. In this chapter I will, however, proceed as if premise 1 is true. Most authors who discuss incompatibility claims do likewise.

Some theologians and philosophers of religion deny premise 2. Dewi Zachariah Philips argues that religious utterances are more concerned with the sphere of human conduct and experience than with making truth claims. He even suggests that his view defuses any conflict with psychological explanations of religious belief because the latter restrict the possibilities of what religious utterances mean.[21] Like philosophers who deny that scientific theories are aimed at truth, deniers of premise 2 constitute a minority position among professional philosophers.[22] Minority positions can be true but a discussion of the arguments for them falls beyond the scope of this chapter. I will go along with the majority positions here and accept premises 1 and 2. It is worth noting that if one of both minority positions is true, no incompatibility argument gets off the ground.

Premise 3 is the vital premise in the argument. As it is stated, premises 1 and 2 say nothing about which CSR propositions and religious propositions are in potential conflict.[23] It should be noted that it is difficult to make a case in which religious propositions that form the core of most religious traditions conflict with CSR theories. No proposition stated by CSR theories conflicts with propositions like "God (or another supernatural being) exists," "Jesus rose from the dead" or "people's souls are immortal." The religious propositions that are in potential conflict with CSR propositions are more peripheral, as we will see below. It therefore seems that an incompatibility argument, if sound, will not do a lot of damage for many religious believers. They can nonetheless create some damage and the damage might be greater for some traditions than for others.[24]

Existing incompatibility claims appear to target three substantial supernatural beliefs. Dawkins and various popular writers suggest that the incompatibility is obvious and therefore they do not elaborate on their claims. I take it that their argument is best cashed out as an incompatibility argument between how CSR theories state that religious beliefs are formed (i.e., through natural selection and various cognitive mechanisms) and how religious believers believe they are formed. Popular writers suggest that CSR shows us the *real* causes why people hold religious beliefs and that these *real causes* differ from the causes claimed by religious believers.

Another candidate for conflicting propositions is another claim about how people come to hold religious beliefs. Gijsbert van den Brink argued that CSR theories could conflict with the claim that religious beliefs result from divine revelation.[25] Many religious traditions claim that people come to hold religious beliefs as a result of some divine revelation. CSR theories by contrast show that religious belief comes naturally and requires no revelation.

Helen De Cruz raises a final incompatibility argument. According to De Cruz what we learn from CSR theories makes it doubtful that humans can successfully engage with God through rituals.[26] The claims in question are incompatible because the etiology described in the CST & HPC (see sections 3.2.1 & 3.2.3) shows that rituals were selected by natural selection.[27] Furthermore, they were selected for vastly different reasons than engaging with God. For example, on the HPC, ritualized actions are by-products of standard responses to fear and threats; on the CST, rituals are means of signaling trustworthiness. De Cruz argues that this etiology does not fit well with an Anselmian conception of an almighty omnibenevolent God.[28] She writes, "Under the assumption that God is omnibenevolent, it is peculiar that God would engage with us, using these particular mechanisms. Why would God use mechanisms that result in outgroup hostility, warfare, and terrorism?"[29] These phenomena imply what De Cruz calls "sinister factors," like anxiety and fear.[30] She argues that rituals involve sinister factors by referring to Will Gervais[31] and Hall et al.,[32] who argue that rituals lead to outgroup hostility, and to Scott Atran,[33] who argues that rituals lead to acts of terrorism.[34]

Premise 4, two conflicting propositions cannot both be true, hinges on the logical law of noncontradiction. The law is accepted by a large majority of philosophers. A minority denies that the law always holds and allows for true contradictions. They sometimes refer to Buddhist and especially Jain philosophers. Some Jain philosophers hold the view that reality is always perceived differently from different points of view. They deny that any point of view can claim to represent the complete truth. Instead, all views together comprise the truth. Since some points of view might contradict others, contradictions can be true.[35]

Recently, some philosophers revived this idea in a position known as "dialetheism."[36] Defenders of dialetheism could claim that religious propositions and scientific propositions can be seen as different points of view that may contradict. Apart from the fact that dialetheism is highly controversial, denying premise 4 does not obviously help. Modern-day dialetheists certainly do not claim that all contradictions are true, they only allow for some true contradictions.[37] The well-known paradoxes of self-reference are their main examples. Dialetheists only allow for a small number of contradictions and it is not clear whether they would allow a contradiction between a religious and scientific proposition.

4.4 Criticizing the Argument(s)

As mentioned before, the crux of the argument lies in premise 3. (Some of the propositions stated by CSR theories conflict with propositions which religious believers, as religious believers, hold to be true.) From here on I assume (for the sake of the argument) that the other three premises are true and I focus solely on premise 3, which can be criticized in two ways. The more obvious way is responding against a specific incompatibility claim. Some have argued that there is no conflict between what CSR theories show and the Christian claim to revelation.[38] Others have argued against the conflict suggested by popular writers.[39] A second kind of response is more general and aims to deny the very possibility of any incompatibility. I first discuss the specific responses and then the more general ones.

4.5 Specific Responses

In Section 4.3 I mentioned three specific incompatibility claims:

(1) The conflict of causes. CSR theories claim that religious belief is caused by cognitive mechanisms and evolutionary pressures

while religious believers claim it is caused by a supernatural being.
(2) The role of revelation. CSR theories claim that religious belief arises intuitively and religious believers claim it arises as a result of revelation.
(3) The role of rituals. CSR theories claim that religious rituals serve an evolutionary function while religious believers claim they are means of engaging God or other supernatural beings.

In what follows I argue that none of these claims hold water.

(1) The conflict of causes. CSR theories claim that religious belief is caused by cognitive mechanisms and evolutionary pressures while religious believers claim it is caused by a supernatural being.

The first belief targeted is a meta-belief about what causes people to hold religious beliefs. Gijsbert van den Brink responds that the causes laid bare by CSR are not the whole causal story. He argues that God can make use of cognitive mechanisms to let himself be known. He compares it to how Christian missionaries made use of Roman roads to spread the Christian faith across the empire. While one can rightly claim that the spread of Christianity was caused by Roman roads, claiming that its spread can solely be attributed to Roman roads goes way too far.[40]

Peter van Inwagen offered a similar response. In his discussion of Paul Bloom's work, he notes that the causes of religious belief to which CSR theories point need not exclude that supernatural agents causally interact with humans.[41] He writes, "If there are supernatural agents it does not *follow* that the explanation of the fact that human beings believe in them has no evolutionary component. . . . Naturalistic explanations of supernaturalistic belief offered by naturalists like Professor Bloom . . . tend to convey the implication that they are 'all the explanation there is.' But this implication is not logical."[42] Van Inwagen argues that the explanations offered by CSR theories can easily be accommodated in a supernaturalistic framework.⁴³ He does not give a detailed description of what this supernaturalistic framework is. It would likely involve God, or other supernatural beings, being registered by the cognitive mechanisms discussed in CSR theories. He thus argues that there is no conflict between claims made in Bloom's theory and the claim that there exists something supernatural.

Van Inwagen's argument is above all one for compatibility between (propositions implied by) Paul Bloom's theory and theism. He does not indicate whether his claim can be expanded to cover more specified substantial supernatural beliefs and different CSR theories. I note that most religious traditions do not make many detailed claims about the causes of religious belief. Most merely claim that religious belief is caused by contact with one or more supernatural beings.⁴⁴ Van Inwagen's argument can thus accommodate most religious traditions. His argument can also accommodate other CSR theories. In Chapter 2 we distinguished adaptationist theories and cognitive bias theories.⁴⁵ Few problems arise for cognitive theories. Most supernatural beings people in major religious traditions believe in have the ability to make use of people's cognitive mechanisms. They can trigger the agency detection device like other agents do, do moral actions to trigger the moral dyad or cause meaningful experiences to trigger the existential theory of mind. The mechanisms that feature in the preparatory account are harder to exploit. I described, however, that the biases in the preparatory account do not produce religious beliefs but make humans prone to see teleology and believe in ontologically diverging things. Therefore, they cannot be seen as causes of religious belief but merely as preparers of the way. Evolutionary theories suggest that religious belief is caused by evolutionary pressures. This proposition can easily be wedded to supernatural causes if the supernatural being is believed to be responsible for, or able to control, the evolutionary process. In many religious traditions people believe that a supernatural being created the universe and everything in it. A being that created the world could easily have set up the evolutionary process in such a way that people have religious beliefs. In this way this being indirectly causes religious belief. Other, smaller supernatural beings cannot be said to cause religious belief by setting up the evolutionary process. For example, supernatural beings like demons or demigods lack the power to do so because they did not create the world. By consequence there might be a conflict between substantial supernatural beliefs about smaller, non-creating supernatural beings and adaptationist CSR theories.[46]

Kelly Clark and Justin Barrett offer a different response. They argue that what CSR theories show fits well with the Christian tradition of the *sensus divinitatis* (SD). The idea goes back to Thomas Aquinas and John Calvin. Alvin Plantinga gave the best-known recent defense. He argued that God could have implanted a cognitive device in humans to let himself be known.[47] Clark and Barrett note that CSR and the SD tradition agree that

(i) religious belief is formed immediately without inference;
(ii) religious belief is (nearly) universal; and
(iii) religious belief is hard to shake.[48]

Clark and Barrett add that the idea of the *sensus divinitatis* has to be reformulated to some extent to fit the data of CSR, but the general idea is the same. For example, they note that some CSR theories state that supernatural beliefs emerge with greater detail while on most accounts of the *sensus divinitatis* they are rather vague.[49] Clark and Barrett state that the causes laid bare by CSR theories can coexist with a supernatural cause who indirectly causes religious beliefs by implanting the required cognitive mechanisms in humans. Their response is only valid when theories that refer to a cognitive mechanism are taken into account. In adaptationist CSR theories there is no mention of cognitive mechanisms that could have been implanted.[50] This response is also only valid for supernatural beings with the ability to create; in this case they need to have created humans with the required cognitive mechanism(s). Clark and Barrett make a more substantial claim in their response than the one I discussed above. Just like Van Inwagen's response, Clark and Barrett's argument suffices to deny incompatibility between CSR causes and (most) supernatural causes. However, they need to take a more substantial and more controversial claim[51] (i.e., the claim that there is a *sensus divinitatis*) on board.

We thus have two responses to the first incompatibility claim: one response states that (most) supernatural beings can make use of cognitive mechanisms or evolutionary processes to cause religious beliefs; the other states that supernatural beings implanted cognitive mechanisms in humans or made them evolve. Although there might be a problem for belief in smaller, non-creating supernatural beings, the first incompatibility claim does not seem to harm many beliefs.

(2) The role of revelation. CSR theories claim that religious belief arises intuitively and religious believers claim it arises as a result of revelation.

We noted a second incompatibility claim, namely, between the CSR claim that religious belief is formed naturally, without much need for instruction, and the religious proposition that religious beliefs result from revelation. This claim resembles the first but is different since the previous claim makes no reference to revelation. This claim (if correct) will not harm all religious traditions equally. The concept of revelation is much more important in Christianity than in other traditions. Eastern religious traditions put more emphasis on the importance of intuitively formed beliefs.

As to religions where revelation is (very) important, a good response is to refer to the tradition of general revelation. Christian thought knows a distinction between special and general revelation. Special revelation is often considered God's revelation as it was recorded in the Bible. Hugh Ross defines general revelation as "information about God and His plan for humanity that comes from considering the creation, or nature, the tangible expression of His divine nature and character."[52] Jeroen de Ridder and René van Woudenberg write,

> God reveals himself to all human beings in at least two different ways—through the works of nature that present themselves to the

human senses, and through human conscience. . . . The guiding idea is that when humans observe and inspect the cosmos, either with the naked eye, or through telescope and microscope, they are in effect facing the manifestations of divine majesty, effects of divine activity, instantiations of God's power. And when humans reflect on what they ought and ought not to do, on what is good and what is bad, on what is valuable and what is not, they will, when all goes well, think thoughts that are in effect divine revelations of God's will.[53]

Although some theologians are critical about the value of general revelation,[54] it is widely accepted in Christianity. General revelation is easily expanded to include information about God (or gods) that comes naturally through cognitive mechanisms. Some of the responders I mentioned earlier refer to theistic evolution to match the evolutionary history of religious belief with God's activity. They also reinterpret God's activity as activity through secondary means instead of through direct action. A similar response is on offer against this claim.

(3) The CSR proposition that religious rituals serve an evolutionary function is incompatible with the religious proposition that rituals are means for engaging with one or more supernatural beings.

Helen De Cruz argues for incompatibility between the evolutionary function of religious rituals and the function claimed by religious believers. De Cruz's argument can be understood in two ways. She herself emphasizes the poor fit between a claim to God's omnibenevolence and the sinister factors in CSR theories of rituals. Her argument resembles the well-known problem of evil.[55] The sinister factors to which De Cruz refers are anxiety (hazard precaution theory), uncertainty (costly signaling), and wishful thinking. Anxiety and uncertainty certainly worried older defenders of the problem of evil,[56] so pointing to those does not add much to the problem of evil. Wishful thinking is generally considered a bad way of forming beliefs but it is not clear whether it is also evil. Evil is usually understood as involving suffering or moral evil. Wishful thinking does not obviously lead to suffering or moral evil.

It is therefore not clear whether De Cruz's claim adds much to older defenses of the problem of evil.[57] Several responses to the problem of evil have been proposed.[58] Since De Cruz's claim appears to add little to the problem, these responses might serve as responses to De Cruz's argument as well.

Rather than trying to respond to the problem of evil, I note that CSR theories of religious rituals need not involve the sinister factors that De Cruz alludes to. The authors De Cruz refers to do not make a convincing case that ritual behavior necessarily involves sinister factors. Hall et al. do not refer to the CST and Gervais only mentions it in a reference. Gervais tries to explain an outgroup bias toward atheists by referring to the BGT. The BGT holds that believing in big gods fostered pro-sociality. Gervais argues that the theory suggests that people who do not believe in big gods (nowadays most of these are atheists) will be expected to act less pro-social and hence be discriminated against. His argument can be expanded to the CST by claiming that people who do not engage in costly displays will not be (or will be less) trusted because they do not signal adherence to pro-social norms. The expansion is, however, not obvious. According to the BGT, belief in big gods has the function of enforcing pro-social norms. It predicts that societies with this belief will cooperate more and better. The CST operates much more on the individual than on the societal level. By performing costly rituals an individual can signal to others that she is committed to pro-social norms and hence is a reliable cooperator.[59] Since it operates more on the individual level, the CST does not predict that people from one society (or group) will have an ingroup bias. It at best predicts that people will prefer to cooperate with people who engage in costly rituals and might hold them in higher esteem. It does not predict hostility toward people that do not engage in costly rituals. The claim that religious rituals foster terrorism, as Atran suggests, goes too far. Acts of terrorism are quite rare and are not pro-social acts.

De Cruz does not refer to Harvey Whitehouse's theory of identity fusion. According to identity fusion, joint participation in intense rituals can fuse individuals together into very closely knit communities.

De Cruz could argue that very closely knit communities will be more prone to ingroup bias and outgroup hostility. Again, I argue that this need not be the case. First, sinister consequences are not guaranteed by partaking in intense rituals. Whitehouse clearly states that identity fusion can have beneficial effects.[60] He is, however, not clear about when it has sinister or beneficial consequences. Maarten Boudry argues that the theory needs to take the content of beliefs into account.[61] If Boudry is right, sinister consequences of identity fusion can be avoided by avoiding sinister beliefs. Even if identity fusion easily has sinister consequences regardless of the content of beliefs, religious traditions can take measures to avoid them. Religious leaders can encourage dialogue with outgroups or closely monitor participants of intense rituals. Sinister consequences of identity fusion can likely be avoided.

The argument can also be understood in a second way as a conflict between propositions about why people perform rituals. While CSR theories suggest people do so for evolutionary reasons, religious traditions maintain they perform them to engage with God (or other supernatural beings). The religious reasons for performing rituals need not conflict with evolutionary reasons. One way to respond is claiming that the function of rituals changed over time. It is possible that people started doing costly rituals for their evolutionary use but that this practice was later incorporated to serve religious purposes as well. Many religious feasts used to be harvest festivals and were only later invested with an explicit religious meaning. An example is the Jewish feast of Sukkot. According to the book of Exodus, the feast started as a harvest festival.[62] Later, the feast became dedicated to remembering the exodus from Egypt.[63] Clearly, the motives for engaging in rituals can change and this need not cast doubt on their sincerity.

The incompatibility could also be resolved by distinguishing good and bad reasons for performing rituals. From a Christian point of view, the evolutionary reasons can be considered hypocritical reasons for performing rituals. A distinction can be made between those who engage in rituals to signal honesty or other virtues and those who do it to get closer to God.[64]

4.6 General Responses

Others objected to the very possibility of *any* conflict between CSR theories and religious beliefs. Some build on the more specific responses I discussed above. We can distinguish three responses in the debate over CSR. The most obvious response is denying incompatibility by claiming that an argument misrepresents or misunderstands the supernatural belief under discussion. A second response denies incompatibility by claiming that CSR claims and religious beliefs are on a different level of explanation. A third response rephrases the targeted supernatural belief.

The first response denies incompatibility by claiming that the argument misrepresents or misunderstands the belief or CSR claim under discussion. Since religious traditions and scientific explanations are complex and few scholars are experts in both fields, showing a conflict is difficult. Mistakes can easily be made. The alleged conflict between the CSR claim that religious belief is caused by various cognitive mechanisms and the religious belief that it is caused by God is an example. Some popular writers, like Dawkins, do not clarify how cognitive mechanisms cause supernatural beliefs and therefore do not show why there is a conflict. They also do not elaborate on what religious believers actually believe about the causes of their beliefs. Instead, they assume that a belief in God as cause means the belief that God causes supernatural belief directly without any mediation like cognitive mechanisms. This conflict results from misrepresenting both what religious traditions claim and what CSR theorists claim. This response casts doubt on any quick claim to an incompatibility between CSR theories and (the content of) religious beliefs.

Jonathan Jong defends another response. Jong argues that supernatural beliefs and CSR claims are on a different level of explanation.[65] Justin Barrett and Ian Church make a similar but less elaborate argument.[66] Jong distinguishes at least three levels of explanation. He distinguishes between cognitive explanations and evolutionary explanations of religious belief—the former being proximate explanations and the latter ultimate. Proximate cognitive explanations show the cognitive mechanisms by means of which a religious belief is formed in an individual's mind and ultimate, evolutionary explanations explain why these cognitive mechanisms were selected in the first place. Jong distinguishes an even more ultimate level of explanation. He notes that some theological explanations aim to explain why evolution occurred at all and why there is life.[67] As an example he refers to the cosmological argument. The argument seeks to establish that God is the ultimate cause of the universe and everything in it. If the argument is successful, theists can claim that God worked through natural processes to cause religious belief. Jong does not give a verdict on the cosmological argument or other ultimate theological explanations.[68] He merely aims to show that no incompatibility is possible because religious propositions and CSR propositions function on different levels of explanation.

Apart from its dependence on the success of natural theology, the major problem with Jong's response is that it only evades *some* incompatibility claims. It can show that there is no conflict between supernatural activity (in the production of religious beliefs) and evolutionary processes. It can, however, be of little aid for incompatibility claims about why rituals are performed or about the role of revelation. Furthermore, it is not clear that putting religious propositions at a more ultimate level will remove all incompatibilities. The proposition that God used violent evolutionary processes to make sure humans have the right cognitive mechanisms for religious belief seems to conflict with the Christian proposition that God is omnibenevolent. The evolutionary process is characterized by survival of the fittest and a lot of suffering. As De Cruz argues, claiming that God used this evolutionary process does not square well with the idea that God is omnibenevolent. The conflict boils down to the old problem of evil to which I referred above. Again I lack space and time for a thorough discussion of the problem of evil. My point is that Jong's response might not solve all incompatibility problems or could raise new ones.

A third general response tries to resolve incompatibilities by reinterpreting and rephrasing supernatural beliefs. Many responders rephrase the targeted religious propositions in such a way that the conflict disappears. In doing so they make use of the rich hermeneutical possibilities of their (usually Christian) religious traditions. Kelly Clark and Justin Barrett's claim that what we learn from CSR theories fits well with the tradition of the *sensus divinitatis* can be regarded as one such response. When reconciling the idea with CSR data they note that the CSR data do not fit entirely. Clark and Barrett note that CSR theories do not agree with Plantinga's claim that religious belief is formed under tranquil or thoughtful conditions.[69] Barrett's HADD and Bering's EToM suggest instead that the conditions are mostly ignorance and terror.[70] The data from CSR theories also do not support the claim that religious belief is innate, as Calvin believed.[71] Responding to the alleged incompatibility between CSR and revelation also follows this strategy. While the idea of general revelation is old, it did not include the experiences that trigger CSR mechanisms or beliefs shaped by natural selection. Traditionally, it meant that God's existence is apparent in his creation.[72] Incorporating the experiences that trigger cognitive mechanisms or beliefs that evolved is not a far stretch from the original idea but it is applied in a new way.

What the limits of this strategy are is hard to assess. If CSR propositions were to target core tenets of a religious tradition, like the belief that there is a supernatural being or the belief that Jesus rose from the dead, reinterpretation is harder. The propositions targeted by specific incompatibility claims I discussed in this chapter did leave room for reinterpretation and many others likely will too. Future incompatibility claims should thus be mindful of the complexity and richness of religious traditions and this increases their burden greatly.

4.7 Conclusion

The incompatibility arguments inspired by CSR theories do not hold water. I noted, unlike some other authors, that there is no obvious incompatibility between CSR theories and religious belief. I also argued that the alleged conflicts (between the causes of religious belief, revelation or natural religion, and the role of rituals in CSR theories or religious traditions) can be resolved. I also discussed some general strategies for responding to incompatibility arguments. Some of them might also be useful for refuting future incompatibility arguments. For now, we can conclude that there is no real threat that propositions of CSR theories are incompatible with religious propositions. The epistemic status of religious belief thus remains unharmed so far.

5

Arguing for Unreliability

5.1 Introduction[1]

In contrast to the arguments in Chapter 4, which were largely underdeveloped and unarticulated, a number of authors present elaborate arguments for the conclusion that religious belief is unreliably formed. Unlike incompatibility arguments that only targeted three substantial supernatural beliefs, unreliability arguments, if successful, do more damage. The arguments aim to show that *most* supernatural beliefs people hold are unreliably formed and therefore epistemically tainted.

In this chapter, I distinguish four kinds of unreliability arguments. I argue that they either fail to make a case for unreliability or need not affect the status of supernatural beliefs.

5.2 What Is the Argument?

Unreliability arguments that rely on CSR theories take the following generic form:

(1) CSR theories show that the mechanisms that produce supernatural beliefs are unreliable.
(2) Beliefs that are produced by unreliable mechanisms suffer from a serious epistemic deficiency.
(3) Therefore, supernatural beliefs suffer from a serious epistemic deficiency.

All unreliability arguments I discuss in the next sections follow this general schema. The main differences lie in how they argue for premise

(1). Some conclude to unreliability because CSR theories show that the mechanisms for supernatural belief were shaped by natural selection. Others argue that CSR shows that the mechanisms produce many false god-beliefs. A related argument states that the mechanisms produce mutually incompatible beliefs. A final argument concludes to unreliability because supernatural beliefs result from misattributions made by cognitive mechanisms. Before discussing these arguments in more detail I move to some clarificatory remarks about the existing arguments.

5.2.1 CSR

All unreliability arguments I discuss below refer to one or more CSR theories in one of their premises.[2] One author, Robert Nola, also refers to Sigmund Freud's theory of projection. All arguments I discuss below refer to the HADD. One refers to the EToM and to the COT. One argument refers to the BSPT and the BGT. The caveat I made in Chapter 2 that caution is in place when arguments rely on these theories holds for all arguments I discuss in this chapter. Though this might cast doubt on the unreliability arguments, I will not pursue this line any further in this chapter.

Some authors claim that their argument also works if other CSR theories are plugged in. Nola sees his unreliability argument as a general schema that can include a number of theories.[3] Wilkins and Griffiths ambitiously claim that all contemporary evolutionary explanations of theistic belief hypothesize that theistic belief is unreliably formed.[4] Braddock also suggests his argument does not depend on a specific theory.[5] Because CSR theories are sometimes very different, this is not as easy as these authors claim. Below I will show that not all CSR theories can be fitted in to unreliability arguments.

5.2.2 Epistemic Deficiencies

The *epistemic deficiencies* mentioned in the second premise can be manifold. Braddock draws the conclusion that theistic beliefs are rendered *unjustified* by scientific theories.⁶ Nola concludes that theistic beliefs are *debunked*.⁷ Wilkins and Griffiths write that debunking arguments should *undermine our confidence* in theistic beliefs.⁸ Goodnick concludes that theistic beliefs are *unwarranted*.⁹ Clark responds to "arguments that claim to demonstrate that evolutionary psychology *undermines rational belief* in God."¹⁰

Being unjustified, being debunked, being undermined, being unwarranted, and being irrational are not the same. All have been the subject of extensive philosophical analysis. A survey of all falls beyond the scope of this chapter. Nonetheless, these qualifications all give a negative verdict on the epistemic quality of a belief. Therefore, all unreliability arguments conclude to some serious epistemic deficiency of supernatural belief. In the remainder of the chapter I will not opt for one of these negative qualifications and leave it at epistemic deficiencies.

In what follows, I discuss five unreliability arguments. Before I do so, I will discuss one common response to all unreliability arguments in Section 5.3. In Section 5.4 I discuss two evolutionary unreliability arguments; in Section 5.5, I discuss an argument that claims CSR mechanisms produce many false god-beliefs; and in Section 5.6 I discuss a similar argument that claims the mechanisms produce incompatible beliefs. Finally, in Section 5.7, I discuss an argument that claims that CSR mechanisms result from misattributions.

5.3 Reasons to the Rescue

A common response against unreliability arguments is what I call the "reason response."¹¹ In its summarized form, it states that whether CSR mechanisms are reliable or not (often) does not matter because religious believers have other reasons for religious belief at their disposal.

Jonathan Jong and Aku Visala offered the most elaborate defense. They argue that unreliability arguments¹² fail to distinguish the context of discovery and the context of reasons. Jong and Visala argue that while unreliability arguments might show that supernatural beliefs *originate* from an unreliable cognitive mechanism, they do not show that supernatural beliefs are wholly *sustained* by this mechanism. Jong and Visala argue that supernatural beliefs can be sustained by independent evidence and arguments. Their examples of independent evidence are arguments from natural theology.[13] Other examples of extra evidence could be religious testimony. Because CSR mechanisms do not explain how people form supernatural beliefs based on additional evidence or arguments, unreliability arguments only do harm to "unreflective epistemic agents."[14]

Justin McBrayer makes a similar claim. He argues that unreliability arguments[15] do not and cannot tell us whether supernatural belief is *all things considered* justified. Whether a subject is justified in holding supernatural beliefs depends on whether she has (1) alternative evidence for the belief and (2) new evidence available for the belief. When a subject learns that the mechanism that produces her supernatural beliefs is unreliable, she can (1) reflect on whether she has other evidence or (2) try to find out whether there is any evidence out there that could support her belief.[16]

I argue that the reason response has only a limited range and is not obviously valid. Jong and Visala cede that unreliability arguments will still harm unreflective epistemic agents. How many subjects are harmed therefore depends on what it takes to be a reflective epistemic agent. If being a reflective epistemic agent requires knowledge of contemporary natural theology, as Jong and Visala suggest, many religious believers will not meet the standard.[17] Many, if not most, believers do not know about recent arguments from natural theology and very few have studied them thoroughly. More believers could meet the standard if religious testimony is included as additional evidence.

If justification depends on additional evidence or reasons then the justification becomes dependent on the force of that evidence and reasons. If justification depends on arguments of natural theology, the arguments need to be valid. If justification depends on religious testimony, the testimony needs to be reliable. No consensus on arguments of natural theology appears to be in sight.[18] There is also ample discussion over the reliability of religious testimony.[19]

An additional reason to doubt the validity of the reason response is that the force or persuasiveness of additional reasons might be dependent on CSR mechanisms. Helen De Cruz and Johan De Smedt survey a number of arguments from natural theology and claim that CSR mechanisms can (partly) explain why people find them convincing. For example, the fine-tuning argument would rely on the bias for promiscuous teleology (see Section 2.3.4).[20] If this is the case, there is no clear separation between the context of discovery and the context of justification for supernatural beliefs. The justification by arguments from natural theology might ultimately depend on CSR mechanisms and therefore do little to rectify their unreliability.

McBrayer's appeal to evidence that is out there is controversial and counterintuitive. McBrayer relies on an externalist account of justification where a belief can be justified by factors (like evidence) outside of the believer's mental life. Not only is externalist justification controversial,[21] but it is obviously not true that the external evidence justifies supernatural belief, as I argued in the previous paragraph.

Jong and Visala note that defenders of unreliability arguments fail to distinguish between whether one *is* justified and whether one *could* be justified.[22] This observation counts *against* the reason response rather than in favor of it. While no argument I discuss below indeed concludes that supernatural belief cannot merit a positive epistemic status, this was not the goal of its defenders. Some defenders explicitly claim that supernatural belief can be rescued by theistic arguments if these are cogent.[23] Therefore, defenders of the reason response seem to agree with defenders of unreliability arguments.[24] Both appear to have different goals. Defenders aim to show that supernatural belief often suffers from serious epistemic deficiencies while adherents of the reason response aim to defend the overall justification or rationality of reflective theistic beliefs. This suffices to show that the reason response is not a good reply to the unreliability arguments to which I will now turn.

5.4 Evolutionary Unreliability Arguments

5.4.1 Goodnick's Evolutionary Unreliability Argument

The most popular unreliability arguments are evolutionary unreliability arguments. Arguments of this kind are defended by Liz Goodnick and by John Wilkins and Paul Griffiths. The two arguments differ considerably from each other. I discuss Goodnick's argument first because hers is the most straightforward. She writes:

> Beliefs caused by HADD + ToM + EToM + MCI [i.e., the Cognitive Optimum HvE] are caused by faculties that were selected for by natural selection. Faculties that were selected for by natural selection are, first and foremost, selected for their facilitation in survival and reproduction—not because they attempt to represent the truth. Because religious beliefs are not caused by a belief-forming mechanism aimed at the production of true beliefs, they should not be trusted. The beliefs they produce are unwarranted for the same reason beliefs based on wish-fulfillment are unwarranted: even if they happen to be true, it will be because the believer "got lucky" in this case.[25]

Goodnick's argument can be stated as follows:

(1) CSR shows that the mechanisms that produce supernatural beliefs were selected by natural selection.
(2) Mechanisms selected by natural selection are primarily aimed at survival and not at truth.
(3) Mechanisms that are not primarily aimed at truth are unreliable.
(4) Therefore, CSR shows that the mechanisms for supernatural beliefs are unreliable.

Goodnick rightly notes that (many) CSR theories state that the mechanisms at the root of supernatural belief were selected by natural selection.[26] Combined with the premise that natural selection selects primarily for survival success and not for truth, she concludes that the mechanisms responsible for supernatural belief are unreliable and its resulting beliefs unwarranted.

To my knowledge, no author has responded directly to Goodnick's argument. Some have offered responses to similar arguments they constructed themselves.[27] They deny that an evolved mechanism cannot be primarily aimed at truth. Justin Barrett and Ian Church argue that a cosmos-designing god could have appropriately tuned the mechanism(s) responsible for religious belief to make himself known.[28] Kelly Clark and Justin Barrett claim that God could have implanted the mechanism responsible for religious belief.[29] Alvin Plantinga makes the same argument.[30] They claim that, because it was guided by God, evolution can select for mechanisms that are aimed at truth. It can, because, for the responders, evolution is not a blind process aimed solely or even primarily at survival; in their view evolution is to some extent guided by a god. Clearly their responses rely on a form of theistic evolution. Theistic evolution does not deny that evolutionary processes are usually aimed at survival. It adds that a god sometimes directs or tweaks the evolutionary processes or that a god laid out the path of evolution in a particular direction. This move defuses the debunkers' unreliability claim because on theistic evolution the mechanism can be primarily aimed at truth. By arguing in this way, these authors deny the second premise of our first evolutionary unreliability argument.

Another response objects premise (2) as well. It does not resort to theistic evolution but argues that the claim—namely, that belief-forming mechanisms, which were selected by natural selection, are not aimed at truth—is too general. Many (if not most) of our belief-forming mechanisms were selected by natural selection. These include our sense perception and common sense and maybe even our ability to do science. Goodnick's argument could thus do a lot more damage than she intends: its conclusion leads to what might be called "evolutionary skepticism." Evolutionary skepticism also casts doubt on Goodnick's own premises since they were likely formed by common sense. Another evolutionary debunking argument proposed by John Wilkins and Paul Griffiths attempts to evade this problem. I now move to their argument.

5.4.2 Wilkins and Griffiths's Evolutionary Unreliability Argument

Wilkins and Griffith propose a different evolutionary unreliability argument. They argue for the following:

(5) Mechanisms that were selected by natural selection can either be constrained by reality or not.
(6) If they are constrained by reality they are reliable.
(7) If they are not constrained by reality they are unreliable.
(8) CSR shows that the mechanisms for supernatural beliefs are unconstrained by reality.
(9) Therefore, CSR shows that the mechanisms for supernatural beliefs are unreliable.

Unlike Goodnick, these authors do not claim that natural selection taints all belief-forming faculties. They accept that natural selection does not primarily select for truth but add that this does not force the conclusion to evolutionary skepticism. Evolutionary skepticism can be defeated by linking evolutionary success to true belief. If they are linked, natural selection will favor organisms with true beliefs.[31] Wilkins and Griffiths thus start with a suspicion of skepticism of any evolved belief-forming process.[32] Unlike Goodnick, they leave room for a possibility of overcoming the skepticism.

They go on to argue that in the case of many common-sense beliefs, true belief (or rather having true beliefs) is linked to evolutionary success. Wilkins and Griffith call the link a "Milvian Bridge."[33] They define a Milvian Bridge as follows:

> *Milvian Bridge*: X facts are related to the evolutionary success of X beliefs in such a way that it is reasonable to accept and act on X beliefs produced by our evolved cognitive faculties.[34]

Applied to common sense, they argue that common-sense facts can be related to the evolutionary success of common-sense beliefs in such a way that it is reasonable to accept and act on common-sense beliefs. They argue that if most common-sense beliefs were false, survival would be difficult. If an animal or human were to act as if the world is a certain way when the world actually is that way or similar to it, its actions will be successful. If it acts as if the world is a way and the world is, in fact, not that way, its actions will be unsuccessful and will be a waste of resources.[35] Having true common-sense beliefs is thus evolutionarily beneficial whereas having false common-sense beliefs is not.

Wilkins and Griffiths, however, do not go as far as claiming that common-sense beliefs match reality. They argue that common-sense beliefs can be accepted and acted upon but they are not as tolerant for common-sense concepts. They elaborate:

> Our commonsense concepts are themselves an evolutionary inheritance, and we know that they differ systematically from those of other animals. So it is plausible that if our evolution had followed a different course, we would have a different conceptual scheme. It is possible to see in this observation grounds for another kind of evolutionary skepticism. . . . The commonsense way in which humans see the world has no more or less ontological authority than the ways in which other animals see the world.[36]

They refer to the physicist Arthur Eddington. He contrasted the common-sense belief that tables are solid objects with the scientific belief that tables are areas of mostly empty space. From a common-sense point of view, it makes sense to claim that the table is solid. From a scientific point of view the best that can be said is that the probability of his elbow sinking through the surface was small enough to be neglected for the purpose of writing his lecture (Eddington 1930).[37] Wilkins and Griffiths note that an obvious rejoinder is that a belief in solid tables is a mere illusion and that, in fact, there are no solid tables. Their response is ambiguous, as they write:

> But there is no reason to abandon the world of commonsense, as long as we are prepared to accept that we are not the only animal whose evolved perceptual and conceptual schemes can stand alongside the measurement and conceptual schemes of science, and be explained by

it. There really are red things and green things, but there are also things which have ultra-violet colours that we cannot detect but other animals can. There are many ways of classifying the world which are *not purely arbitrary* and . . . the fact that these classifications are *constrained by reality* explains why they have some degree of pragmatic utility.[38]

In this response Wilkins and Griffiths seem to move from a claim that common-sense beliefs are true to a claim that common-sense beliefs are not purely arbitrary and constrained by reality. They add that our cognitive faculties evolved because they track truth in the human "Umwelt." As to scientific beliefs they claim its status does not depend on the reliability of the cognitive mechanisms that produce them. They claim that the methods of science, data, and arguments of scientists give us ample reasons to believe their conclusions.[39]

Wilkins and Griffiths's argument for a Milvian Bridge for common sense boils down to a claim that common-sense beliefs can be considered not purely arbitrary and constrained by reality because of the pragmatic success they yield. No such Milvian Bridge is available for the mechanisms that give rise to supernatural belief because CSR theories do not refer to the truth of supernatural beliefs when they explain their effect on reproductive fitness.[40] Since these theories show that supernatural belief can be produced without it being true (because they are adaptations or by-products). They therefore show that supernatural cognition is not sensitive to reality in the same way sense cognition is.

Wilkins and Griffiths entertain the possibility of religious noncognitivism where supernatural beliefs need not be about something but are mere expressions or ways of life (see also Chapter 3). They also allow for a possibility how supernatural beliefs can be saved by natural theology.[41]

Wilkins and Griffiths's claim—that supernatural beliefs do not yield pragmatic success and hence no Milvian Bridge is available for the mechanism that produces them—is problematic. I argue that they are wrong and a case for pragmatic success of supernatural belief can be made. Humans do not run into supernatural beings like they bump into solid tables. Contact with supernatural beings (if they exist) is more indirect. The pragmatic success of supernatural belief lies in the spiritual fruits it delivers. Supernatural beliefs can lead to greater spiritual fulfillment and a life of increased sanctity. This fact shows that supernatural beliefs are not purely arbitrary and are at least constrained by some reality. For my argument, I draw on an argument made by William Alston who argued that supernatural beliefs allow for a test of sanctity. Alston made his claim as part of a broader defense of the rationality of religious experiences. His main claim is that religious experiences[42] resemble sense perception in important regards and should therefore enjoy the same (or a similar) epistemic status. He notes that, at first glance, sense perception seems different because it allows for a test. Sense perception provides a "map" of the physical and social environment and enables us to adjust our behavior accordingly and it enables us to anticipate events. The map allows us to test the outputs of sense perceptions and corrects them where they go wrong. Religious experiences cannot be tested by a map of the physical and social environment. However, Alston claims they can be tested by a map of the divine environment. The divine environment allows for a test of sanctification. When the outputs of religious experiences lead to a life of greater sanctity, they can pass the test.[43] In this way, Alston shows that supernatural beliefs can make a claim to pragmatic success. Their success can consist of a life of greater sanctity. Greater sanctity can help people flourish. If supernatural beliefs were to lead to a life of lesser sanctity or more evil, people would function less well. In this case, one could claim that their supernatural beliefs are frustrated by reality as well.

I have thus far claimed that the outputs of the mechanism responsible for supernatural belief can make the claim to pragmatic success Wilkins and Griffiths demand. My claim is, however, not yet sufficient. The debunker can still drive a wedge between the pragmatic success of sense perception and that of supernatural belief. She can claim that the pragmatic success of sense perception is much greater. Sense perception allows for scientific beliefs. Their pragmatic success is a lot more impressive than that of supernatural beliefs. The success of scientific beliefs ranges from space rockets to cures for diseases. Its impressive success makes it very unlikely that beliefs resulting from sense perception are not aimed at truth. By comparison the success of supernatural belief appears meager. This route is, however, not open for Wilkins and Griffiths. They appear to deny that scientific beliefs depend on human cognitive mechanisms that produce common-sense beliefs by claiming they rely on the data and arguments scientists give.[44] When assessing the pragmatic success of supernatural beliefs, the comparison should be limited to common-sense beliefs.

The difference can be framed in another way that avoids reference to scientific beliefs. The debunker could claim that a world where humans lack sense perception will be a very different world. People will be unable to navigate their environments and there will not be technological innovations. A world without mechanisms for supernatural belief would be far less different. Maybe people then would lead a life of greater sanctity and subjectively feel closer to God than without such mechanisms. However, the difference would clearly be less noticeable than the absence of sense perception, though. It is thus far less clear what difference or what use supernatural beliefs make. In response, I don't see why supernatural belief should have the same degree of pragmatic success as sense perception does. It suffices that supernatural beliefs yield considerable pragmatic success. Wilkins and Griffiths deny that supernatural belief has any success at all. Alston shows that this is not the case. Furthermore, the difference supernatural belief makes should not be underestimated. Christianity clearly had a profound influence on Western societies. Hinduism and Buddhism shaped the Indian subcontinent and spiritist beliefs influenced large parts of the world. While the difference supernatural belief makes might not be as great as the difference of beliefs resulting from sense perception, its impact is surely big.

Additional evidence for my claim to pragmatic success for supernatural beliefs is that some supernatural beliefs can fail. In the case of perceptual beliefs, some will be discarded because they do not live up to the test of the environment. Someone who forms the belief that walls are penetrable will be kept in check when she hits her first wall. The belief can be said to lack pragmatic success because it resulted in failure to navigate the environment. In the case of supernatural belief, some beliefs will be discarded for lack of pragmatic success as well. Examples are beliefs in premodern fertility cults. After the rise of city-states they lost their ground because they were unable to make sense of people's needs. They thus failed to cope with the (new) environment.

Another way in which Wilkins and Griffiths could respond is by accepting that supernatural beliefs are constrained by some reality but add that this reality is not God or any supernatural being. Spiritual fruits could be the result of reduced stress by making time for religious practices or a larger social network by being a member of a religious group. The burden of proof is on defenders of the unreliability arguments to show that they are. Wilkins and Griffiths have not done so.

Wilkins and Griffiths also suggest a different way to argue that the mechanism behind supernatural belief is unconstrained by reality.[45] They discuss how another belief-forming mechanism can make a claim to a Milvian Bridge, namely, common sense, and argue that the mechanism behind supernatural belief does not resemble it sufficiently. Apart from issues of vagueness, this argument is problematic because the comparison is limited. If a mechanism does not resemble formation of common-sense beliefs, it does not follow that the process is unconstrained by reality. A better way to rank the mechanism for supernatural beliefs under unreliable processes is by comparing it to a belief-forming mechanism we know is unconstrained by reality. I will do so by making a comparison to the self-serving bias.

The self-serving bias is a clear example of a belief-forming mechanism that is (largely) unconstrained by reality. Keith Campbell and Constantine Sedikides define the self-serving bias as "[a tendency for] taking credit for personal success but blaming external factors for personal failure."[46] The bias thus makes people prone to believe that they deserve all praise for personal successes and do not deserve blame for personal failures.[47] Campbell and Sedikides review evidence for the claim that counterevidence to personal merit and external blame is very easily discarded or rationalized. Especially in situations of perceived threat people's beliefs persist.⁴⁸ Campbell and Sedikides thus provide clear evidence that the beliefs resulting from the self-serving bias are unconstrained by reality. Sander Koole notes that biases like the self-serving bias often serve to ward off negative emotions like anxiety. He also claims they serve the larger goal of emotion-regulation. These are defensive responses, which protect the individual from changing her outlook.⁴⁹ From Campbell and Sedikides and Koole's discussion of the self-serving bias I derive the following characteristics of belief-forming mechanisms that are unconstrained by reality. They

(i) are insensitive to counterevidence;
(ii) ward of negative emotions; and
(iii) have a rather fixed outcome.

The first is to be expected for belief-forming mechanisms that are unconstrained by reality. If a mechanism is unconstrained by reality its operations will not be altered by evidence from reality. Its operations will also be insensitive to evidence that is not from reality, for example, false or confabulated evidence, but this is irrelevant for our purposes. The mechanism responsible for supernatural beliefs does not meet the first criterion. Of the three theories Wilkins and Griffiths refer to, HADD, unambiguously, has an important role for evidence in the production of supernatural beliefs. We noted how Barrett argued that supernatural beliefs can be formed after experiences of things like wispy forms (see Section 2.3.5). There are also independent reasons to think that supernatural beliefs and how they are formed are sensitive to evidence. People sometimes report life-changing religious experiences that gave their lives a radically new direction. There are also ample examples of people coming to belief in supernatural beings. Therefore, supernatural beliefs and how they are formed do not appear to share the first characteristic.

The second characteristic stems from the observation that biases are defense mechanisms. They defend people against perceived threats and allow them to function better. In a way biases like the self-serving bias lead people to believe that states of affairs are better than they are in reality. While evidence against personal merit or for external merit can lead to feelings of failure or anguish, the self-serving bias makes sure that feelings of self-worth survive. In short, it makes people feel better. The mechanism behind supernatural belief does not unambiguously make people feel better. We noted in Chapter 2 how supernatural beings are often believed to have a moral concern. This might put demands on people that they perceive as burdensome. Therefore, supernatural beliefs and how they are formed do not appear to share the second characteristic either.

The third characteristic is that mechanisms that are unconstrained by reality produce rather similar beliefs that are not subject to much change. The self-serving bias only has belief in personal merit and external blame as output. Furthermore, the beliefs are not subject to much change. This fits well with mechanisms unconstrained by reality because the beliefs are not shaped or changed by reality. Clearly, supernatural beliefs can differ to some extent depending on the experience an individual has had. Supernatural beliefs also often change over time. Alston noted that sometimes an increase in sanctity can be observed in supernatural beliefs. Therefore, supernatural beliefs do not seem to share the third characteristic either.

I conclude that both evolutionary arguments are unconvincing. Goodnick's argument suffers from obvious flaws. Wilkins and Griffith's argument, though more intricate, also does not hold water upon scrutiny.

5.5 False God-Beliefs Unreliability Arguments

Matthew Braddock proposes a different unreliability argument. He claims that the mechanism responsible for supernatural belief is unreliable because it produces many false god-beliefs. His argument is the following:

(10) Polytheistic beliefs and finite god-beliefs are false god-beliefs.
(11) CSR mechanisms have disposed us humans to such god beliefs across ordinary environments and throughout human history.

(12) So, CSR mechanisms have disposed us humans to a large percentage of false god-beliefs across ordinary environments and throughout human history (from (10) and (11)).
(13) Given (12), we should suspend judgment about the reliability of CSR mechanisms in ordinary environments with respect to the class of god beliefs, unless we have independent evidence favoring reliability.
(14) We have no independent evidence favoring the reliability of CSR mechanisms in ordinary environments with respect to the class of god beliefs.
(15) So, we should suspend judgment about the reliability of CSR mechanisms in ordinary environments with respect to the class of god beliefs (From (13) and (14)).[50]

Braddock's conclusion (15) is slightly different than the conclusions from the arguments I discussed above. He merely concludes that we should be agnostic about the reliability of CSR mechanisms; the arguments above concluded that the mechanisms are shown to be unreliable. It is not immediately clear whether agnosticism about the unreliability of a belief-forming mechanism implies a serious epistemic deficit of the beliefs it produces. One could argue that the burden of proof is on the one who argues against the reliability of a mechanism. Those who have a stricter take on the matter might argue that the burden of proof is on the defender.[51] Braddock's expanded argument (see below) shows that he belongs to the stricter camp. I will not take a stance on this matter and go along with Braddock and the stricter camp in this section. In this regard, Braddock's conclusion comes very close to the conclusions of the arguments above.

His first premise makes clear that Braddock takes false god-beliefs to be non-monotheistic god-beliefs. According to monotheism, there is only one God. If monotheism is true, then polytheistic beliefs must be false. He adds that many nontheists will also accept the premise, and even many polytheists too, if the premise was changed only slightly to "The vast majority of polytheistic and finite god beliefs are false."[52]

With premise (11), Braddock notes that the mechanisms laid bare by CSR theories dispose humans to having polytheistic beliefs and finite god-beliefs. Braddock argues for this point at length. In his discussion of (11), he is less firm. He writes, "Various lines of converging evidence *suggest* that CSR mechanisms have disposed us humans to polytheistic and finite . . . god beliefs *throughout the human past*."[53] His use of "suggest" reminds us of the caveats against relying on CSR data I noted in Chapter 2. His phrase "throughout the human past" reveals that much of the alleged false outputs of CSR mechanisms are to be situated long ago in human history. Braddock discusses how polytheistic and finite god-beliefs were prevalent among ancestral humans. He then refers to a version of the BGT to argue that monotheistic beliefs are a recent innovation.[54] Braddock thereby suggests that an assessment of (un)reliability should look at the whole evolutionary history of a mechanism. It is far from clear that such a requirement is needed. If we would apply this logic to our perceptual faculties, we would note that they too produced many false beliefs. For a good part of human history, people formed the belief that the earth was flat and that the sun revolved around the earth based on perception. If we follow Braddock's requirement, we should conclude that perception produces a lot more false beliefs and is a lot more unreliable. It makes much more sense to assess perception by looking at how many false beliefs it produces in the present. If we assess CSR mechanisms in the same way, we note that nowadays they produce a lot more monotheistic beliefs and the case for (11) is less strong.[55]

Braddock also refers to other CSR theories than the BGT to argue for (11). He refers to Justin Barrett and Paul Bloom who both state that polytheism is more natural or intuitive than monotheism.[56] Premise (11) is probably correct on a number of CSR theories. However, some CSR theories do seem to predict more monotheistic beliefs. The MDT predicts belief in an ultimate moral agent (see Section 2.3.6 in Chapter 2); the EToM predicts belief in an ultimate meaning-giver; and the BGT predicts belief in big gods. Furthermore, Barrett also claims that the human ToM produces intuitive beliefs in super properties like omniscience that fit much better with monotheistic beliefs.[57] Although the truth of premise (11) is not established, there are reasons to think that some CSR mechanisms produce more polytheistic and finite god beliefs. For this reason, I will grant (11) in the rest of this section.

I also will not dispute premise (14), or Braddock's conclusions (13) and (15). I merely note at this point that Braddock's argument is not an argument for the conclusion that supernatural belief is unreliably formed. It merely concludes that the mechanisms laid bare by CSR theories are unreliable. The unreliability of CSR mechanisms might be overcome by other forces that shape supernatural beliefs. Braddock acknowledges this point and expands his argument with the following:

(16) CSR mechanisms operating in ordinary environments are significant contributors to the god beliefs of past and present humans (CSR's empirical thesis).

(17) If we should suspend judgment about the reliability of significant contributors to a belief-forming process P with respect to a class of beliefs C, and we have no good reason to think other significant contributors would confer reliability upon P with respect to C, then we should suspend judgment about the reliability of P with respect to C.

(18) We have no good reason to think other significant contributors to our belief-forming processes would confer reliability upon them with respect to the class of god beliefs.

(19) So, we should suspend judgment about the reliability of our belief-forming processes with respect to the class of god beliefs (from (15) to (18)).

(20) If we should suspend judgment about the reliability of a belief-forming process P with respect to a class of beliefs C, then we are not justified in holding a particular belief B that is both produced by P and falls into class C, absent independent evidence for B.

(21) So, we are not justified in holding our god beliefs, absent independent evidence for them (from (19) and (20)).[58]

I will contend (18) and argue that there is reason to think that other significant contributors to supernatural belief can confer reliability. I thus grant for the sake of the argument that the mechanisms can be judged unreliable (although I claimed that the case for (11) is not as strong as Braddock argues), but I hold that such unreliability need not affect all supernatural beliefs. A number of CSR theorists acknowledge that the mechanisms they discuss do not work in isolation but always work in a cultural context. Though they do not give details, they leave it open that cultural input can give further direction to supernatural belief. Will Gervais and Joseph Henrich, for example, note that most CSR mechanisms cannot explain why people used to believe in ancient gods like Zeus but do not anymore. To explain this, culture must be taken into account.[59]

A similar point was also raised by Aku Visala and David Leech. They write,

> It is not, in fact, the case that the standard model [the Cognitive Optimum, HADD, EToM, HvE] gives us a complete account of the existence and persistence of particular and content-specific theistic beliefs. . . . There are far more mechanisms involved in particular belief formation than are specified by the standard model. Even if it turns out that the cognitive mechanisms that the standard model posits are unreliable, the irrationality of theism does not follow. In other words, if the standard model catches only some causal pathways through which the theist's beliefs come about, then it is perfectly possible that the other pathways are rational. This is enough, we claim, to dismantle the unreliability arguments as they stand now.[60]

Visala and Leech's response is not exactly the same as mine.[61] They argue that the mechanisms laid bare by CSR are only one pathway among others that lead to supernatural beliefs. The other pathways remain unaffected by the alleged unreliability of CSR mechanisms. In my response, I argue that the unreliability of CSR mechanisms can be overcome by other factors.

Braddock did not claim that the mechanisms laid bare by CSR theories are wholly unreliable. From a monotheist perspective, they occasionally produce true god-beliefs, namely, monotheistic beliefs. Cultural input, like education, study, or growing up in a religious community, can work on the initial outputs of the mechanism and redirect them to jointly produce monotheistic beliefs.

A comparison to the mechanisms responsible for moral beliefs is helpful. Evolutionary biologists and evolutionary psychologists argue that our moral beliefs are rooted in our biological nature. Some have discussed mechanisms that make us altruistic. Examples are reciprocal altruism and kin selection.[62] According to defenders of reciprocal altruism, organisms engage in altruistic behavior because they expect other organisms will act altruistically toward them. Without this reciprocity, altruism cannot survive. Defenders of kin selection argue that organisms engage in altruistic behavior to help the survival odds of related organisms. Since they are related, they share a great deal of genetic material. In helping them, an organism thus helps shared genetic material. Apart from altruistic tendencies, organisms also have selfish tendencies. Above all, most organisms will look out for their own survival and reproduction. The selfish tendencies will likely produce moral beliefs that are usually considered false. The altruistic tendencies will also produce beliefs many will consider false. Reciprocal altruism will likely produce an ingroup bias whereby members of one's own family or tribe are favored over others. Reciprocal altruism can produce the belief that one should only help another if she will return the favor. This does not force the conclusion that our moral faculties are unreliable and its outputs should not be trusted. This concludes to moral skepticism and makes any outrage over war or genocide uncalled for, as clearly, its outputs can be cultivated by moral education or context.

This all goes to show that although initial outputs can lead to many false god-beliefs, the deficiency can be overcome. Two factors that can bear on religious belief are upbringing and cultural context. Someone who grows up in a monotheistic household and lives in a cultural setting where most people are monotheists is more likely to become monotheistic herself. Influence of upbringing and cultural context can come in two forms. A child can be instructed with words, for example, by religious education. A child can also be influenced by seeing outward religious behavior. Research by Jonathan Lanman and Michael Buhrmester showed that exposure to CREDs (Credibility Enhancing Displays) predicts theism, certainty of God's existence, and religiosity.[63] CREDs are outward behaviors that clearly indicate that someone is strongly committed to a belief.[64] Examples are engaging in rituals, praying before each meal, or wearing religious symbols. Outward behavior by people who are monotheistic can make people more likely to become monotheistic themselves.

I thus conclude that while Braddock makes a good case for the unreliability of CSR mechanisms, he did not make a good case that this affects supernatural beliefs. He did not take into account other contributors to supernatural beliefs that could overcome the unreliability of CSR mechanisms.

5.6 Incompatible God-Beliefs Unreliability Arguments

Another reason why the mechanism responsible for supernatural belief might be judged unreliable is because it produces incompatible beliefs. CSR mechanisms appear to produce both the belief in monotheism and infinite gods and the belief in polytheism and finite gods. Since monotheism is the belief that there is only one god, it is logically incompatible with polytheism, the thesis that there are multiple gods. A belief that god(s) is (are) finite is also incompatible with a belief that god(s) is (are) infinite. A mechanism that produces incompatible beliefs will produce many false beliefs and can thus be judged unreliable. To my knowledge this argument has not been defended at length. Matthew Braddock mentions it but argues it is less promising than his own debunking argument. He writes,

> Why does the argument need to rely on the falsity of polytheistic and finite god beliefs when the diversity of god beliefs already establishes

many incompatible (and thus false) god beliefs? The main reason for relying on (10) [Braddock's premise that CSR mechanisms produce god-beliefs HvE] is that doing so enhances the strength of the argument's case against reliability. The incompatibility established by religious diversity only implies that at least some god beliefs are false. That is not enough to doubt reliability. Premise (10), on the other hand, helps generate the requisite level of doubt. To appreciate this, suppose that there are in fact many finite gods. When we add to this the empirical premise that most god beliefs have been of the polytheistic and finite sort, it is no longer clear that our natural god belief-forming mechanisms are off track.[65]

The argument goes as follows:

(22) CSR shows that the mechanisms for supernatural beliefs produce many incompatible beliefs.
(23) Mechanisms that produce many incompatible beliefs are unreliable.
(24) Therefore, CSR shows that the mechanisms for supernatural beliefs are unreliable.

Despite the shortcomings to which Braddock points, arguing that the mechanism is unreliable because it produces incompatible beliefs has the benefit that it need not take a monotheistic or naturalistic perspective. Braddock's own argument I discussed above rests on the claim that the mechanism produces many finite and polytheistic god-beliefs. From a monotheistic and naturalistic perspective these beliefs are judged false. This argument need not take any perspective.

This argument rests on the claim that mechanisms that produce incompatible beliefs are unreliable. A mechanism that produces incompatible beliefs will always produce some false beliefs. This follows from the logical law of noncontradiction. Apart from a few voices of opposition,[66] the law of contradiction is widely accepted. However, claiming that the mechanism produces some false beliefs is not sufficient to judge it unreliable. An unreliability judgment requires that the mechanism is error prone, or produces *many* false beliefs. The mechanisms responsible for supernatural belief we discussed in Chapter

2 do indeed appear to produce many polytheistic, finite god-beliefs and also many monotheistic, infinite god-beliefs. So they produce many false beliefs.

Still, we can claim that the mechanism is not wholly unreliable and needs cultivation in order to arrive at true beliefs. There is yet another response possible, which denies that the mechanism produces many incompatible god-beliefs. I will claim that although the mechanisms produce supernatural beliefs, a belief that a supernatural being is a god requires more.[67] In my response, I do not accept the claim that the mechanisms responsible for supernatural belief produce many finite and polytheistic *god*-beliefs. I do accept that the mechanisms produce beliefs in a multitude of supernatural beings but these beings need not be considered gods. These supernatural beings can be considered gods and thus lead to a polytheistic worldview. However, they can just as well be considered as intermediary supernatural beings, like angels or demons, and be fitted in with a monotheistic worldview. In this framework, the incompatibility between polytheistic belief and monotheistic belief is due to how the beliefs produced by the mechanisms are *considered* or *interpreted*, not because of how the mechanisms operate. Therefore, incompatible god-beliefs (or rather supernatural beliefs) cannot be attributed to the mechanisms.

The incompatibility argument has a mistaken view of what beliefs CSR mechanisms produce. The beliefs produced by CSR mechanisms are rather vague. They produce beliefs that some supernatural being exists or that some supernatural being is like this or that. For example, the EToM produces the belief that some supernatural being is communicating something through a meaningful event. It does not produce the belief that this supernatural being is a god or that the being is (in)finite. The moral dyad produces belief that some supernatural being is responsible for a morally significant event. It also does not produce the belief that there is only one god that causes these events or that that being is (in)finite.

None of the CSR mechanisms produces detailed substantial beliefs like "the Trinitarian God exists" or "Vishnu descended in the form of a tortoise." Detailed beliefs of this kind require cultural input and more interpretation. Justin Barrett notes that cognitive theories of supernatural belief focus on cross-culturally recurrent ideas (and practices). Focusing on Christianity, he claims that many components of it consist of only small elaborations on the cross-culturally recurrent ideas. On the other hand, some Christian ideas deviate. Examples are the idea of God as absolutely sovereign or God as all-knowing.[68] Barrett points to a gap between what cognitive mechanisms yield and the more elaborate, concrete beliefs people hold. I argue that what cognitive mechanisms yield does not suffice to make a distinction between "supernatural being" and "god." A mechanism can produce beliefs that some supernatural being exists and also beliefs about that being's nature. Classifying that being as a "god" requires more. In some traditions, a multitude of supernatural beings will be considered gods and a polytheistic worldview will emerge. This was the case in ancient Rome and in some strands of Hinduism. In other traditions, only one supernatural being will be considered a god. Other supernatural beings will have an intermediary status; they are not considered human or gods. This is the case in Christianity where many supernatural beings are considered angels or demons and in Islam where many are considered jinn.

A similar story can be told about beliefs in God's infinity or finiteness. Like judging a supernatural being to be a god, judging one to be (in)finite requires more than what CSR mechanisms deliver. None of the CSR mechanisms I discussed in Chapter 2 produce the belief that God (or an intermediary supernatural being) is finite or infinite. Some CSR mechanisms do appear to produce beliefs about the might or power of supernatural beings. For example, the EToM and Moral Dyad seem to produce beliefs in supernatural beings capable of bringing about large events. Judging that a supernatural being is finite or infinite usually requires further reflection or argument.

My response to incompatible unreliability arguments differs from my response against false god-beliefs arguments. Before, I granted the unreliability of the CSR mechanisms but argued that they can be corrected by other input (like culture or upbringing). Here, I did not grant the unreliability that CSR mechanisms are accused of. I deny that the production of both monotheistic and polytheistic beliefs or finite and infinite god-beliefs can be attributed to the mechanisms. Here the root of the incompatibility lies in other factors like culture or upbringing. This raises an interesting point. Whereas factors like culture or upbringing can correct false god-beliefs, they can also lead people astray. The factors can thus be both a source of epistemic good and of epistemic bad. I certainly cannot shed light on when these factors are a benevolent influence and when they are malevolent in this chapter and I doubt whether sufficient and necessary conditions for doing so can be found at all. I merely note that in both cases extra input on top of the CSR mechanisms can defeat unreliability arguments and this suffices for now.

5.7 Misattribution Unreliability Arguments

A last argument for unreliability looks closer at the proximate causes of religious beliefs. Defenders of the argument say that CSR theories show religious beliefs result from a misattribution.[69] The argument is more straightforward than the previous one and goes as follows:

(25) CSR theories show that supernatural beliefs result from a misattribution.
(26) Beliefs that result from a misattribution are unreliably formed.
(27) Therefore, CSR theories show that supernatural beliefs are unreliably formed.

Although the argument is straightforward, one key term, "misattribution," stands in need of clarification. A misattribution occurs when a subject forms a false belief by misreading events. This is best explained with an example. A well-documented case of a misattribution is the "rubber hand illusion." Multiple studies showed that people can be convinced that a fake rubber hand is their own hand. In the experiments participants were asked to take a seat and both of their real hands were put out of sight. A fake rubber hand was put in sight and an experimenter touched one real hand and the fake rubber hand with similar movements. After a short while—sometimes as short as 10 seconds—participants grew to believe that the fake rubber hand was their own.[70]

The rubber hand illusion is a clear example of a misattribution. Subjects falsely believe that the rubber hand is theirs because their minds misidentify sensory input. In this case, they wrongfully identify sensory input of a fake hand as input of their own hand. The misattribution results in a false belief, namely, "the rubber hand is mine." The experiment does not show that humans often or usually misidentify bodily sensations. It also does not show that humans are bad at forming beliefs about themselves. It does show that the human cognitive apparatus can lead people astray and can produce false beliefs in situations that are similar to the experimental setup.

With the example of the rubber hand in mind, it is clear that beliefs resulting from a misattribution will be unreliably formed. By definition, misattributions lead to false beliefs. On any measure, a belief-forming process that *always* produces false beliefs will not meet the requirements for reliability. Premise (26) is therefore obvious.

Premise (25) is more difficult to establish. Most CSR theories do not straightforwardly suggest that religious beliefs result from misattributions. Many merely claim that religious beliefs result from some cognitive mechanism or that religious beliefs yielded an evolutionary advantage for our ancestors. Sometimes, however, defenders of CSR theories do claim that cognitive mechanisms go astray when they produce religious beliefs. One such claim was made by Stewart Guthrie. Guthrie defends a version of the HADD theory (see Section 2.3.5). Unlike Justin Barrett, Guthrie unambiguously claims that religious beliefs result from "false positives."[71] He claims that the human cognitive system is often misidentifying input for an agent. Importantly, he claims that these misidentifications foster the belief in invisible agents, which in turn leads to belief in gods. A misattribution thus lies at the root of religious beliefs, according to Guthrie.

Other CSR theorists make similar suggestions. The main defenders of the Moral Dyad, Kurt Gray and Daniel Wegner, also suggest that people—or rather their cognitive systems—are making a mistake when they attribute large morally significant events to God. While moral typecasting is appropriate in most moral situations, our cognitive systems overstretch their normal function when they conclude to ultimate moral agents.[72] Jesse Bering also suggests that people mistakenly see meaningful events as communications of an ultimate meaning-giver.[73] Whereas inferring to minds from symbolic interactions is appropriate when applied to humans, Bering suggests that it is not when applied to an ultimate meaning-giver

We have seen the case that some CSR theorists make for premise (25). I will now argue that their case is not well supported. First, Guthrie does not give good reasons to believe that religious beliefs result from a misattribution. His claim that humans are hyperactive in the detection of agents is plausible, but the additional claim that belief in invisible agents results from misattributing agency is far less plausible. If humans are indeed prone to jump to agency conclusions, they will soon learn that they often make mistakes. Usually, they will check their hunches and have a closer look. When they do not find any agent around, they will correct their initial hunch and not form a stable belief that an agent is or was around. Pascal Boyer also claims that beliefs triggered by hyperactive agency detection will be easily overridden.[74] Justin Barrett agrees with Boyer. He argues that hunches of agency must be easily overridden. If they are not, hyperactive detection would lead to survival difficulties and not advantages. He also notes that detecting invisible agents will not give rise to religious beliefs as we know them because other cultural factors that contribute to religious beliefs must be taken into account.[75]

Gray and Wegner also do not make sufficiently clear how moral typecasting leads to religious belief. They do cite evidence that societies with harsher conditions—and thus with more suffering—have a higher prevalence of belief in God. This, however, does not establish that moral typecasting into moral agents and moral patients produces religious belief. It could very well be that causation goes in the opposite direction and that people first believe in a God who can cause natural disasters before they explain large morally significant events in terms of God's agency. If this is the case, people do not infer God's existence to account for disasters, but merely infer God's agency.

Apart from questions as to whether both theories provide a detailed explanation of how religious belief is formed, they also do not show that religious beliefs cannot result from a *correct* attribution. Though detection of agents could be hyperactive and thus prone to error, Guthrie does not show that beliefs in invisible agents and gods result from misattributions. Believers in nearly all religious traditions believe that God or other supernatural beings can make themselves known to humans. The fact that human detection of physical agents is hyperactive does not rule out the possibility that humans can correctly pick up signals from supernatural beings in their environments. In order to show that religious beliefs result from misattributions, Guthrie would need to show that the sensory input which leads to religious beliefs is in fact something natural. He does not do this. In fact, Guthrie gives few details about the input that triggers the HADD. A strong case for misattribution requires a strong case for natural input.

The same holds for Kurt Gray and Daniel Wegner's theory. They do not show that people cannot correctly infer a divine cause of morally significant events. Looking for moral agents is appropriate in many situations. In many, if not most, morally significant situations one or more agents did in fact cause the moral harm or good. In order to argue that moral typecasting goes astray in a given situation, one needs to show—or at least make plausible—that there is no moral agent in that situation. Some religious traditions hold that God does in fact cause natural disasters.[76] God is also often held responsible for situations that are regarded as morally good, like if someone escapes death or has a child. Gray and Wegner could argue that we know the causes of morally significant events and these causes are not God. Earthquakes are caused by seismic waves and escaping death is often caused by medical intervention. This claim does not show that God does not cause morally significant events because God can make use of these natural events to bring something about. Gray and Wegner's theory does not show that inferring to God's activity in these cases is a mistake. Like Guthrie, they appear to assume that there is no ultimate moral agent and therefore that concluding to one is a misattribution.

My last point hints to an inherent feature of CSR theories and scientific theories in general. Usually scientific theories do not refer to supernatural entities in their explanation of phenomena. This practice is known as methodological naturalism. Methodological naturalism is the thesis that scientific theories ought not refer to nonnatural entities to explain phenomena. Applied to CSR, methodological naturalism prevents CSR theories from appealing to anything supernatural to explain how religious beliefs came about. If explanations of religious beliefs cannot refer to anything supernatural, the theories cannot refer to supernatural input. Concluding that supernatural belief results from a misattribution in this way is question begging.

There is discussion over whether methodological naturalism is an intrinsic rule to which scientific theories must subscribe or rather the result of a gradual exclusion of supernatural causality. Maarten Boudry, Stefaan Blancke, and Johan Braeckman defended the latter view. They argue that explanations that rely on supernatural entities proved less successful in the history of science than purely natural explanations.[77] Whether methodological naturalism was indeed the result of greater explanatory power of natural explanations over supernatural explanations makes little difference for our discussion. Even if CSR theorists do not refer to supernatural input for this reason, concluding to a misattribution from CSR theories is still question begging. On Boudry, Blancke, and Braeckmann's view, CSR theories do not show that religious beliefs result from a misattribution. On this version, the plausibility of misattribution claims therefore hinges on the past success of natural explanations and whether their success support metaphysical naturalism—the claim that nothing supernatural exists. This claim goes well beyond the discussion over CSR and is a lot harder to defend.[78]

Methodological naturalism appears to explain why some CSR theorists claim that religious beliefs result from a misattribution. While methodological naturalism casts doubt on existing misattribution claims, it does not make them impossible. For example, a defender of Guthrie's anthropomorphism theory could test whether religious beliefs are often formed after a subject is exposed to natural patterns or sounds of leaves.[79] To support this claim, the defender need not explicitly consider if religious beliefs are caused by supernatural input (if this is possible at all). If enough examples of people forming religious beliefs after misidentifying natural input are documented, we have a strong case for premise (25). At the moment, premise (25) is not sufficiently supported and the misattribution argument fails.

With this in mind, defenders of a misattribution argument could accept that not all religious beliefs result from misattributions and still maintain that HADD is making more misattributions when it produces supernatural belief. Even if not all detected supernatural agents can be ranked under false positives, the mechanism still sometimes leads to beliefs in agents when none are there. The HADD can thus be argued to make misattributions in the detection of supernatural agents and natural agents. If he argues for that, the defender of misattribution arguments compromises the epistemic status of our beliefs in human and animal agents too. In a paper with Ian Church, Justin Barrett makes a similar claim. He claims that any claim that CSR mechanisms are off-track has implications that range far wider than supernatural beliefs. They write,

> Religious beliefs [including supernatural beliefs HvE] are not the only beliefs these faculties [CSR mechanisms HvE] form, however. If they are unreliable when forming metaphysical beliefs about the existence of gods, souls, and the afterlife, are they reliable to deliver true beliefs regarding the features and causal properties of the natural world, the social world, human minds, and moral realities?[80]

Applied to the HADD, especially belief in human minds seems to be compromised if the HADD is judged unreliable. In response to this challenge, defenders of misattribution arguments could grant that the HADD is also off-track when producing belief in natural agents but add that there are additional reasons for holding beliefs about natural agents. They could also respond that when an agent is repeatedly detected, the HADD is more reliable. If they respond in this way, defenders can no longer use HADD's misattributions to argue for a serious epistemic deficiency of supernatural beliefs. I noted when criticizing Braddock's argument that there can be additional reasons for holding supernatural beliefs. The HADD can also repeatedly detect supernatural agents.

5.8 Conclusion

None of the arguments I surveyed in this chapter make a successful case that supernatural beliefs are unreliably formed. One argument, namely Braddock's argument that CSR mechanisms are unreliable because they produce many false god-beliefs, might be able to make the case that the mechanisms laid bare by CSR mechanisms are unreliable. I argued that this unreliability can be overcome.

6

Arguing for Naturalistic Religious Experiences

6.1 Introduction

CSR theories can be put to use in another argument. They could show that religious experiences are naturalistic and hence not caused by anything supernatural. When subjects have putative experiences of the supernatural, they would in fact only experience natural phenomena. Putative religious experiences are a trick or illusion fobbed on us by our cognitive mechanisms. As a result the evidential value of religious experiences would disappear. The argument resembles an older response to the argument from religious experiences.

Like the previous arguments I discussed, it is not immediately clear how the argument(s) goes and what damage it could do to the epistemic status of religious beliefs, if sound. The argument targets only a limited number of supernatural beliefs, namely those that are based on religious experiences. Supernatural beliefs that are based on explicit reasoning or testimony[1] are unaffected.

Below I will discuss the argument in more detail. I argue that the argument is best construed as a counterargument against the argument from religious experience. I argue that the counterargument is not sound because it is not clear that CSR-based explanations are naturalistic and are of a sufficiently wide scope to explain religious experiences.

6.2 What Is the Argument?

6.2.1 The Argument from Religious Experience

Before we can assess how CSR theories could serve in an objection to the argument from religious experience, I will first briefly discuss the argument itself. Defenders of the argument from religious experience argue that religious experiences have evidential value for theism or for the existence of a supernatural being. Some go even further and argue that religious experiences can justify religious belief. The argument has been defended in many forms. In this section, I focus on Richard Swinburne's version because Swinburne's argument has been very influential and is still widely discussed.

I summarize Swinburne's argument from religious experiences as follows:

(1) Subjects have putative experiences of God (or another supernatural being).
(2) During putative experiences of God, it seems as if God exists.
(3) In the absence of counterevidence, subjects are justified in believing that things are as they seem to be.
(4) Therefore, in the absence of counterevidence, subjects who have putative experiences of God are justified in believing that God exists.

I gave examples of reports of religious experiences in Chapter 1. These examples suffice to show that some subjects have putative experiences of God or other supernatural beings. Swinburne himself, however, argues for a stronger claim. He claims that *many* people experienced God or some supernatural being connected to God.[2] In this chapter I focus on beliefs formed after religious experiences in individual subjects and not on the general case for theism like Swinburne does. For my purposes, it suffices that at least some subjects have putative religious experiences.

Premise (2) is drawn from how subjects describe their religious experiences. Religious experiences of this kind are usually described in such a way that they entail the existence of something external according to Swinburne. Experiences of God can also be described in such a way that they do not entail the existence of anything external. For example, a subject could describe an experience as follows: "It seemed to me that God talked to me last night." Describing an experience as how things seemed to a subject merely describe the internal processes during an experience and therefore do not entail the existence of anything external. Swinburne calls these descriptions "internal descriptions." Often, however, subjects describe religious experiences in an external way. For example, subjects often do not merely state that it seemed as it God talked to her last night but that God actually talked to them last night. Swinburne calls these descriptions "external descriptions." Unlike internal descriptions, external descriptions refer to a reality outside of the subject's mind.

To argue for the third premise, Swinburne relies on his "principle of credulity." He notes that generally we regard putative experiences of something as good evidence to suppose that something exists. The putative experience also gives good evidence for the characteristics of that something. For example, when a subject has a putative experience of a table, she has good evidence to suppose that there actually is a table before her. If the table is experienced as being solid, then she also has good evidence to suppose that the table is in fact solid. Swinburne summarizes his principle as follows:

> If it seems (epistemically) to a subject that x is present (and has some characteristic), then probably x is present (and has that characteristic); what one seems to perceive is probably so.[3]

Swinburne adds that apparent memory of experiences can be trusted as well, although memories are less forceful than present experiences.[4]

The principle of credulity applies to experiences of God as well. Therefore, Swinburne can draw the conclusion that putative experiences of God are evidence for the existence of God.[5] Swinburne's remark that many people also have experiences of supernatural beings connected to God (e.g., angels, messengers) suggests that his conclusion can be expanded to include the existence of other supernatural beings as well. The argument only concludes that subjects who have putative experiences of supernatural beings themselves are justified in holding existential or substantial supernatural beliefs. The argument concludes nothing for people who did not. Swinburne, however, adds that putative religious experiences also have evidential value for others. Just like putative experiences can (and ought to) be trusted, testimony can be trusted as well.[6]

According to Swinburne, the most straightforward way to deny the conclusion of his argument is denying that the principle of credulity always holds and adding some additional requirements.[7] He also notes another possible response. Swinburne recognizes that the evidence, which putative experiences yield, can be defeated. He distinguishes four kinds of considerations that can defeat experiential claims. First, an experience can be of a kind that in the past proved to be unreliable. For example, the experience can be had under the influence of drugs and drug-induced experiences usually turn out to be false. Second, an experience can occur under circumstances where similar experiences proved false. For example, if someone saw a text of ordinary font size at great distance, her experience is likely false. The third defeater is evidence that x very likely was not present during the experience of x. For Swinburne, the burden on type 3 defeaters is hard because they need to show that it is very improbable that x was not present to override the force of the putative experience. A fourth defeater is evidence that x very likely was not the cause of the putative experience of x. Such evidence would be a causal explanation of the putative experience of x that does not involve x.[8]

I will not discuss the first three kinds of defeaters in the remainder of this chapter and focus on the fourth kind. In the next section I discuss what a causal explanation of supernatural beings without supernatural beings could be and how CSR theories could provide it. Before I do so, I add that not any causal explanation of a putative experience of x, without x, will be a defeater. An alternative explanation of religious experiences which claims that aliens cause religious experiences will not do. The explanation must also be *more plausible* than the explanation with x. When an explanation is more plausible than a rival explanation is a subject of much debate. I return to this below when I discuss the principle of parsimony.

6.2.2 The Objection from Naturalistic Explanations

I ended the last section with Swinburne's four defeaters for (the evidential force of) religious experiences. In this section I discuss his fourth defeater—evidence that x was very likely not the cause of the putative experience of x—in more detail. Applied to religious experiences, a defeater of this kind is evidence that God or any other supernatural being was not the cause of the putative religious experience. Evidence like this takes the form of a causal explanation that does not refer to anything supernatural as cause. I will call explanations like these *naturalistic explanations*.

A number of authors also made the claim (or similar claims) that naturalistic explanations of religious experiences defeat the evidential value of religious experiences.[9] Their claims are, however, usually underdeveloped. Most of the authors also do not provide sufficient empirical data to show that religious experiences have a natural cause. Others conflate naturalistic explanations of religious experiences with explanations of religious belief.[10] All authors do suggest that naturalistic explanations of religious experiences show that putative experiences of supernatural beings are caused by natural input.

Evan Fales defends a more elaborate argument. He argues that naturalistic explanations for mystical experiences can undo their evidential significance.[11] Fales does not refer to CSR theories but to an explanation by Ioan Lewis.[12] Lewis argues that mystical experiences can be explained as a means to access political and social power or control. Fales argues that Lewis's explanation with social circumstances as the cause of religious experiences is *more powerful* than theistic explanations, with God as their cause.[13] Fales's argument resembles Swinburne's fourth defeater for the argument from religious experience.

According to Fales, Lewis's explanation shows that religious experiences are not caused by God or any supernatural being. As a result, religious experiences lose their evidential value.

Recently, some have used CSR theories to make a similar claim as Fales (or rather to respond to it). Justin Barrett writes, "We have identified the regions of the brain responsible for religious experience and can artificially induce religious experience. Therefore, its causes are entirely natural and so, we have no need to appeal to anything supernatural to account for them. Hence, theistic belief is unjustified."[14] Michael Murray also discusses a similar claim and writes,

> Cognitive psychological accounts of religion can account for the origin of religious belief in a way that makes no reference to and requires no causal connection with supernatural reality. However, properly justified belief requires that the target of the belief be causally connected to the belief itself in certain ways. Since these accounts show us that none of those ways are in fact in play in the origins of religious belief, beliefs so generated are unjustified.[15]

Murray responds by arguing that the causal theory of knowledge[16] is not evidently true. Murray's claim applies to supernatural beliefs rather than religious experiences. Both he and Barrett do suggest that CSR theories can yield naturalistic explanations for religious experiences but do not consider this a problem for religious belief. Both Barrett and Murray are not concerned with assessing the impact of naturalistic explanations of religious experiences on the argument of religious experiences but rather with their impact on the overall epistemic status of religious belief. Below I state an argument that limits the focus on religious experiences.

Finally, some authors discuss a related argument. David Leech and Aku Visala note that a God who makes himself known by naturalistic means could be regarded as a deceptor. They note that religious believers generally feel that they are in a direct relationship with supernatural beings. If supernatural beings are not involved in the proximate formation of supernatural beliefs, that feeling is false.

Therefore, a supernatural being that allows this is deceiving religious believers. This is not consistent with the putative omnibenevolence of the God of classical theism. Leech and Visala's argument does not target supernatural beings that are not seen as omnibenevolent. They respond that CSR theories do not provide the whole causal story of how supernatural beliefs are produced.[17]

6.2.3 The Argument Stated

With the discussion of the previous two sections in mind, I state the argument as follows:

(1) CSR theories offer the most plausible explanation for religious experiences.
(2) CSR theories show that religious experiences are not caused by anything supernatural.
(3) Therefore, religious experiences are not caused by anything supernatural (from 1, 2).
(4) If religious experiences are not caused by anything supernatural, religious experiences do not justify supernatural belief.
(5) Therefore, religious experiences do not justify supernatural beliefs (from 3, 4).

This argument is fairly straightforward, although some premises are controversial. We noted in Chapter 2 that some authors raised doubts about the current state of CSR and thereby about the truth of premise (1).[18] Furthermore, it is possible that other explanations of religious experiences (e.g., the social explanation discussed by Evan Fales) are more plausible than CSR explanations. I will not pursue these points in this chapter and accept that CSR theories of religious experiences are the most plausible explanations of religious experiences on offer.

The CSR theories to which premises (1) & (2) refers are some of the theories explaining religious experiences I discussed in chapter 3. Not all theories, however, make claims about the causes of religious experiences. The studies in which neuroscientists study subjects' brains during religious experiences do not. They merely discuss what parts of the brain light up when participants are subjectively in a state of union with God or recite religious texts. Their findings are only relevant for my discussion here if a "nothing but" claim is added, a claim that religious experiences are caused by nothing but neural activity. Andrew and Alexander Fingelkurts discussed "nothing but" claims in neuroscientific research of religious experiences in detail.[19] They conclude that religious experiences cannot be reduced to neural activity and thereby deny that religious experiences are caused by nothing but neural activity. Furthermore, most nonreligious experiences we know involve some neural activity, yet most of them also have external causes. Even hallucinatory experiences are usually triggered by some external input that is misread or wrongfully computed by the brain and are therefore not caused by nothing but neural activity. Any claim that an experience is caused solely by neural activity requires an explanation for how the human brain can produce that experience all on its own.

Some CSR theories do make claims about the causes of religious experiences. Michael Persinger argues that religious experiences are caused by variations in electromagnetic fields. Changes in magnetic fields would cause small, transient, electrical micro-seizures within the deep structures of the temporal lobe, which in turn cause experiences of supernatural presence.[20] On the predictive coding theory, religious experiences are caused by ambiguous stimuli and a subject's prior beliefs. Because a subject holds (religious) beliefs about invisible beings, ambiguous stimuli are seen as supernatural activity. Marc Andersen unambiguously claims that his predictive coding theory shows that religious experiences involve "false positives."[21] He argues that prior (religious) beliefs make subjects prone to experience supernatural beings where in fact there are none.[22]

Intermediate conclusion (3) follows from (1) and (2) if we accept the principle of parsimony. A religious experience could have a natural cause and a supernatural cause. Adding a supernatural cause for religious experiences, however, makes the explanation less parsimonious. The principle of parsimony[23] states that, all other things being equal, a theory that postulates fewer entities is more likely true. The principle is not without its critics,[24] but is widely accepted. Adding supernatural beings to any CSR theory will make that theory less parsimonious and therefore less likely true.

Premise (4) states the objection to the argument from religious experience that I discussed in Section 6.2.2. As Swinburne noted, we should not conclude that God exists on the basis of a religious experience if we have evidence that God (or any other supernatural being) was likely not the cause of that experience. If we accept premises (1) and (2) along with the principle of parsimony, religious experiences are not caused by anything supernatural but by mere natural phenomena. This would suffice to deny that the principle of credulity holds for religious experiences.

If CSR theories show that religious experiences are not caused by anything supernatural and if they are the most plausible explanations of religious experiences, conclusion (5) follows. If (5) is established, the argument from religious experience is defeated. The conclusion is also bad news for religious beliefs that are based solely on religious experiences. People who form the belief that God exists or that God loves them after some putative experience of God, will no longer be justified in holding that belief if (5) is established. People who have additional reasons, like theistic arguments, can still be justified. It is hard to tell how many religious believers will be affected by the argument since it is often unclear what reasons people have available. It is, however, not unlikely that a large amount relies only on religious experiences.[25]

In the next section, I argue that the argument fails by criticizing premise (2) and premise (1). I argue against (2) that CSR theories have not established that religious experiences are not caused by anything supernatural. In fact, most claims about causes of religious experiences are underdeveloped in all theories I discussed. I also argue against (1) that CSR theories are of sufficiently broad scope to explain most religious experiences. Therefore, CSR theories cannot be claimed to offer the most plausible explanation for religious experiences.

6.3 Objection: What Causes Religious Experiences?

I will criticize premise (2) of the argument and argue that CSR theories do not show that religious experiences are not caused by anything supernatural. I argue that although some theories suggest that religious experiences are caused by natural input, the claims are underdeveloped and likely betray a prior commitment to naturalism. Before I discuss my claim, I criticize another reply that claims religious experiences have supernatural causes at a deeper level.

6.3.1 Objection 1: Fully Naturalistic?

A first problem for premise (2) is that it is not obvious that CSR explanations are fully naturalistic. While Persinger's theory and the PC theory do not need any reference to anything supernatural to offer a proximate explanation of religious experiences, they might have to do so to offer an ultimate explanation. A supernatural being might be needed to explain how the human brain, which is triggered by electromagnetic waves, or the human mind, which engages in predictive coding, came about in the first place. If this is the case, both theories cannot explain religious experiences in a fully naturalistic way. Michael Murray makes a similar point. He writes,

> I, for example, don't think there would be a universe if there were no God. I don't think the universe would be fine-tuned for life if there were no God. And I don't think there would be any actual life, believers, human beings, or religion either if there were no God. I might be wrong of course. But let us remember that it is the person arguing against religious belief that bears the burden of defending [the contrary position]. Good luck to them. I have no idea how one would argue for its truth aside from arguing that I am wrong on the claims noted in this paragraph.[26]

Murray's claim makes premise (2) dependent on the success of natural theology. He alludes to the cosmological argument when he claims that there would be no universe if there were no God, to the fine-tuning argument, and to the design argument from complexity in nature to argue that there would not be living intelligent beings. Murray suggests that all three arguments make it unlikely that explanations based on CSR theories are ultimately naturalistic. If the cosmological argument is sound, a creator god must be added. If the fine-tuning argument or the other design argument is sound, a designer god must be added to the explanation for religious experiences.[27]

While both explanations are not naturalistic, opting for both comes at a price. In both cases much of the explanation for why people have religious experiences is still naturalistic. If the cosmological argument is sound, we need to refer to a supernatural being to explain the origin of the universe but not to account for how the human brain and mind took shape and how they produced religious experiences. Much of the qualitative character of religious experiences is thus not influenced by any supernatural intervention. For example, on predictive coding people have religious experiences of a God who actively intervenes in the world and sends signs. The idea of an intervening God is still entirely due to natural factors. It therefore seems that a subject is no longer justified in believing that there is an intervening God on the grounds of her religious experience. If the cosmological argument is sound, it only leaves room for justification of a very limited belief, namely, that there exists a creator god, on the grounds of religious experiences.

If we accept the fine-tuning argument we get similar problems. While a designer god could have more control over what brains and minds humans have and what religious experiences they produce, this does not hold for the designer god to which the fine-tuning argument concludes. The argument states that a number of physical constants had to be very precisely aligned for life to arise. Defenders of the argument claim that this fact points in the direction of a god.[28] God (or another supernatural being) is thus only needed to explain the alignment of some physical constants in the universe. If the argument is sound, much of the explanation for religious experiences is still natural. The qualitative character of religious experiences is still entirely due to natural factors. A subject will thus at best be justified in believing that some supernatural being arranged the physical constants, but not that that being is interacting with people, is morally concerned, just, etc.

The argument from design in nature does not have these problems. If a plausible case can be made that design in nature can only be brought about by acts of God,[29] it is plausible that God designed human brains and minds just like he did other features of nature. However, the argument from design in nature is more controversial than the previous two arguments. Recent arguments of this kind are known as arguments for intelligent design and have been heavily criticized.[30] The argument is also not popular among philosophers of religion and theologians.[31] Claiming that God is needed at the deeper level to explain why human brains and minds are the way they are thus requires accepting a very controversial argument.

The arguments do, however, cast doubts on the truth of premise (2). The discussion on the first two arguments is far from finished. Murray argues that the burden of proof is on those who argue for naturalistic explanations. If this is the case, the ongoing discussion on the cosmological and design arguments makes premise (2) problematic to some extent. I, however, argued that the objection that God is needed at a deeper level of explanation does not help the defender of religious experiences much.

6.3.2 Natural Causes?

A more promising objection also questions premise (2). It states that CSR theories provide too little details about the causes of religious experiences or that the causal explanation they offer is unconvincing.

Michael Persinger argues that the causes of religious experiences are purely natural variations in electromagnetic radiation. Persinger's causal explanation has been severely criticized.[32] Marc Andersen notes that Persinger's view of the temporal lobe as the seat of subjective experiences of the self is not widely accepted in neuroscience.[33] Christopher French and his team attempted to build a haunted house by manipulating, among other things, the variance in magnetic fields. While subjects did report unusual experiences, there was no correlation with the variance in magnetic fields. They suggest that the unusual experiences might result from suggestion rather than variance in magnetic fields.[34]

Marc Andersen, the main defender of the PC theory, does not convincingly show that religious experiences are caused by natural input. On the theory, what and how a subject experiences depends heavily on her "priors" or beliefs about the world. Andersen claims that a subject's (religious) beliefs about the world will make her prone to have religious experiences (more precisely experiences of seeing supernatural agency). By claiming that a subject's priors make her prone to false positives, Andersen suggests that the priors are false or mistaken. He does not argue why this is the case. He also argues that the elusive and vague nature of religious beliefs makes them harder to revise than other prior beliefs about the world. Finally, he argues that the human mind, guided by prior (religious) beliefs, is triggered into religious experiences by ambiguous input. Andersen does not give much detail about what this ambiguous input is. Other authors who defended similar positions like Andersen do. Neill van Leeuwen and Michiel van Elk refer to anthropological research by Tanya Luhrman in an evangelical church. Congregants were encouraged to engage in activities that make God feel real. For this purpose they sometimes use props. For example, congregants were encouraged to make tea for God or set an additional plate during dinner.[35] Second, they refer to traditional healers among the Zulu people. They summon ancestors through drumming and falling into trance. Third, they refer to practices where people pray in front of a statue. The visual form of the image would trigger experiences.[36] Van Elk and Van Leeuwen hint that the examples show that religious experiences rely heavily on suggestion.[37]

Both Andersen and Van Leeuwen and Van Elk argue that subjects are more prone to suggestion when in a state of sensory deprivation.[38] By engaging in activities like fasting, long meditation, or severe physical movement, subjects have less energy. Having less energy to spend, the human mind will focus on its vital tasks and be less quick to update its internal model. As a result, subjects would suffer from a setback and rely more on previously held priors and be more prone to have religious experiences. The authors do not make clear why subjects would fall back on previously held internal models after sensory deprivation and not continue to use their most recent, updated models.

We can now get a clearer idea of the causal explanation of religious experiences according to PC. A subject has certain prior beliefs about God or other supernatural beings and how they relate to the world. These beliefs guide her experiences by reading certain feelings or outward events as having a supernatural origin. Her beliefs will also make her engage in certain activities that trigger these feelings or events. Sensory deprivation might make religious experiences easier to get. Claiming that religious experiences involve false positives, as Andersen does, appears to rely on the claim that prior (religious) belief that make a subject read feelings or events as supernatural are false. This betrays a prior commitment to naturalism (the claim that nothing supernatural exists), for which the authors do not argue. Without a commitment to naturalism, PC does not show that religious experiences have natural causes. If there is a God, certain feelings and events might very well be caused by God and prior religious beliefs might be accurate guides. Engaging in practices might also be good ways of seeking out God or trying to engage with supernatural beings. Many religious traditions indeed teach that going through certain practices is the right way to seek contact with God or other supernatural beings. Because of its unsubstantiated commitments to naturalism and vagueness over the input, PC does not show that religious experiences are not caused by anything supernatural. Premise (2) is therefore not established and the argument fails.

6.3.3 Objection 2: Too Limited Scope

A third objection can be raised but now to premise (1). It can be argued that the scope of CSR explanations for religious experiences is too limited. All of the explanations I discussed earlier only explain a limited number of religious experiences. Persinger's theory aims to explain experiences of a sensed presence. Michiel van Elk and Andre Aleman argue that PC can explain experiences of a sensed presence, religious hallucinations, and mystical experiences, where the subject feels a loss of ego or identity.[39] Out of the three kinds of religious experiences (sensed presence, mystical experiences, and possession) I discussed in Chapter 1 (see Section 1.5), PC explains two. Van Elk and Aleman attribute mystical experiences to changes in multisensory integration resulting in an altered self-referential processing. For mystical experiences, the relative weighing of extroceptive signals (from outside the body) and introceptive signals (from inside the body) in constructing the sense of the self would lead to a reduced awareness of the limits of a subject's body. Van Elk and Aleman even go as far as to claim that the sense of loss of ego or identity can result from *errors* in weighing signals from the inside and signals from the outside.[40] Van Elk and Aleman mainly explain the loss of ego or identity during mystical experiences. They do not explain why God or other supernatural beings are experienced. They therefore, do not explain why people like Meister Eckhart experience a profound contact with God. They also do not explain experiences of possession.

Although Persinger's and Andersen's theories might get a broader scope and explain other experiences in the future, they did not so far. The explanations might have a too limited scope to explain all or most religious experiences. A thorough assessment of their scope would require empirical data on what religious experiences people have worldwide and how widespread they are. I did not find such data, so assessing the scope is not possible at this point.

As a result, we lack sufficient data to back up premise (1). At most, we can claim that CSR theories offer the most plausible explanations for *some* religious experiences. By consequence no general conclusions about the justification of supernatural beliefs based on religious experiences can be drawn.

6.4 Conclusion

In this chapter, I looked whether CSR theories can furnish an argument against religious beliefs that are grounded in religious experiences.

While I argued that theories could undercut the justification of beliefs by religious experiences by offering naturalistic explanations, I argued that CSR theories do not. CSR theories lack details or data to back up their causal explanations of religious experiences. They also appear to have a too limited scope to explain most religious experiences.

7

Arguing against the Consensus Gentium Argument

7.1 Introduction

A final argument based on CSR theories argues against the consensus gentium argument (CGA). The CGA argues that the wide occurrence of supernatural beliefs is evidence against naturalism. CSR theories could furnish a counterargument by showing that the wide occurrence is due to natural factors and therefore likely to occur under naturalism.

7.2 Preliminaries

In this section, I define the terms "naturalism" and "supernaturalism."[1]

7.2.1 Naturalism

Naturalism is a term used to cover many meanings.[2] In this chapter, I use "naturalism" to refer to the thesis that there is nothing supernatural whatsoever.[3] Usually the idea that there is something supernatural is cashed out as the idea that there are one or more supernatural beings. I discussed what I mean with "supernatural beings" when I defined "supernatural beliefs" in Chapter 1. I argued there that "supernatural being" is best considered as a family resemblance concept but that there are some sufficient conditions. Naturalists also deny the existence of anything supernatural that is not unambiguously a being, like Qi or Brahman.

Naturalists make a stronger claim than atheists. On most definitions, atheists are people who do not believe in God.[4] Naturalists go further and explicitly deny that anything supernatural exists. Naturalism can be cashed out in many ways, like humanism, religious naturalism, or scientism.

7.2.2 Supernaturalism

I use "supernaturalism" to refer to the opposite thesis, namely, that there exists at least one supernatural being or something supernatural. Thus defined supernaturalism is quite vague and it can be cashed out in many, rather different, ways likes monotheism, polytheism, full-blown Christian belief, and many others. All of these imply supernaturalism. Whether supernaturalism can be equated to theism depends on how the latter is defined. Theism is the thesis that there exists at least one deity. If "deity" is a synonym for "supernatural being," "theism" is interchangeable with "supernaturalism." Sometimes spirits, angels, and demons are not considered deities. For example, Christianity (at least in some forms) accepts the existence of angels but claims that there is only one God. Many forms of Islam accept the existence of jinn[5] and uphold a strict monotheism. The vast majority of traditions that accept supernatural beings like spirits or angels also accept a supreme god or supreme gods. Some new age traditions are exceptions. The Faery Wicca tradition emphasizes the intervention of elves, fairies, and spirits in people's lives while it remains largely silent about gods.[6] They would be an example of supernaturalists that are not theists. I choose to focus on supernaturalism because a lot of supernatural beliefs people hold are about spirits and not about deities. The term also has no problems including supernatural forces like Qi and Brahman.

7.3 The Consensus Gentium Argument

The CGA argues that the wide occurrence of supernatural beliefs in the world is evidence against naturalism. The oldest version of the argument in Western philosophy is found in Plato's *Laws* where he writes,

> Cleinias: But is there any difficulty in proving the existence of the Gods?
> Athenian stranger: How would you prove it?
> Cleinias: How? In the first place, the earth and the sun, and the stars and the universe, and the fair order of the seasons, and the division of them into years and months, furnish proofs of their existence; and also *there is the fact that all Hellenes and barbarians believe in them*.[7]

Cicero made the most famous statement of the argument in his *De Natura Deorum*:

> For the belief in the gods has not been established by authority, custom or law, but rests on the unanimous and abiding consensus of mankind; their existence is therefore a necessary inference, since we possess an instinctive or rather an innate concept of them; but a belief which all men by nature share must necessarily be true; therefore it must be admitted that the gods exist. . . . This truth is almost universally accepted not only among philosophers but also among the unlearned.[8]

Both Plato and Cicero appeal to universality and thus to an actual consensus among people. In this form the argument does not hold water because there is no actual consensus. Recent versions do not appeal to a consensus but rather appeal to the wide prevalence of religious beliefs.[9] Defenders of modern versions also do not phrase the CGA as a deductive argument like Cicero did but make a claim about the statistical likelihood of finding a wide occurrence of supernatural beliefs. They claim that a wide occurrence is more likely under a form of supernaturalism than under naturalism. The claim is an instantiation of a more general claim, which states that wide occurrence of a belief, is evidence for the truth of that belief.[10] Most defenses and criticisms of the CGA go back and forth between this more general claim and the more specific claim applied to supernatural beliefs. In my discussion of the support and criticism of the CGA below, I will not make a sharp distinction between both.

Alvin Goldman notes that consensus is neither a necessary nor a sufficient condition for knowledge.[11] The same holds for a belief that is widely shared. We cannot conclude from the fact that a belief is widely shared that this belief is true. Nonetheless defenders of the CGA argue that there are good reasons why a widely held belief is evidence for the truth of that belief. Some have argued that the best explanation for a consensus (or a high prevalence of a belief) is that the belief is knowledge.[12] Loren Meierding argued that it is more probable that a belief that is widely shared is true than false.[13] Thomas Kelly argues that the best explanation for a belief that it is widely shared is that the belief is true.[14] In what follows I will follow Meierding in arguing that a wide occurrence of supernatural beliefs makes supernaturalism more probable than naturalism rather than making an inference to the best explanation. My reason is that inferences to the best explanation suffer from some well-known shortcomings.[15] Arguing for increased probability is also clearer.

Cicero's statement of the argument makes clear that the CGA relies on a wide occurrence of *supernatural beliefs*. I noted that the term "religious beliefs" is broader and includes many beliefs that are not directly about supernatural beings or their nature. Most recent versions of the CGA do use the term "religious beliefs." Since religious beliefs that are not supernatural beliefs—like the belief that offerings should be made on a daily basis or that a child becomes part of the Christian community by being baptized—do not support the probability of supernaturalism, For this reason, I will use the term "supernatural beliefs." Cicero's statement also suggests that existential supernatural beliefs are the more important. Modern versions also appear to argue that the belief that one or more supernatural beings *exist* makes some version of supernaturalism more probable. Substantial supernatural beliefs—like the belief that God is loving—would support a different conclusion, namely, that there probably exists a loving God. Since arguments based on substantial supernatural beliefs will rely on a less wide occurrence of those beliefs, I will focus on the standard CGA that relies on existential supernatural beliefs.

I state the CGA as follows:

(1) There is a wide occurrence of supernatural beliefs.
(2) All other things being equal, a wide occurrence of supernatural beliefs is more probable under supernaturalism than under naturalism.

(3) Therefore, all other things being equal, supernaturalism is more probable than naturalism.

Apart from its immediate obviousness, premise (1) is also well established by empirical data. A recent survey based on more than 2,500 censuses, surveys, and official population registers showed that 83.7 percent of respondents reported they had a religious affiliation.[16] Not all people who claim to have a religious affiliation have supernatural beliefs. For example, some Buddhist traditions are naturalistic and in Western Europe some people claim to be Christians but don't believe the Christian God exists.[17] Yet it seems plausible that the vast majority of the religiously affiliated share a commitment to the supernatural belief that at least one supernatural being exists.

The second premise (2) is more controversial. Below I will discuss an objection based on CSR theories in more detail. For now, I distinguish three related reasons why a wide prevalence of supernatural beliefs is evidence for supernaturalism over naturalism[18]:

- Self-trust transfers to trusting others and therefore we should trust that others are usually telling the truth.
- A wide prevalence of a belief would reflect people's experiences and evidence.
- A wide prevalence of a belief is less surprising if that belief is true.

7.3.1 Reason 1: Self-Trust and Trust in Others

A first reason for trusting a wide prevalence of (supernatural) belief is that epistemic self-trust transfers into trusting other. Linda Zagzebski argues for this reason at length. Zagzebski notes that people tend to trust their own epistemic qualities and indeed should do so. Most people have a desire for truth.[19] In addition, they also have a natural belief that the desire can be satisfied. Trusting our epistemic faculties (and the beliefs they produce) is thus the state people start off with when they engage in their epistemic endeavors. According to Zagzebski, this epistemic self-trust is even inescapable. First of all, a case for the reliability of one's own epistemic faculties cannot be made in a noncircular way.[20] She adds that the inescapability of circularity is not the deepest reason why we need epistemic self-trust. The deeper reason is the assumption that there is a connection between getting at truth and our methods of answering our questions (i.e., our epistemic qualities). Without epistemic self-trust we are forced to accept that there is no connection between reasons and truth because our reasons are supplied by our epistemic qualities. By consequence, all our strivings for getting to truth will be in vain. Zagzebski relies on the intuition that trying hard to get at truth (she calls this epistemic conscientiousness) implies a better chance of succeeding. Without basic self-trust trying hard cannot get off the ground.[21]

Zagzebski continues that epistemic self-trust cannot be consistently upheld if we fail to grant others epistemic trust. By using one's own epistemic powers one can come to believe that other humans have the same desire for truth and the same epistemic powers. Since others are similar to us, there is no reason to doubt the trustworthiness of others.[22]

7.3.2 Reason 2: Other People's Experiences and Evidence

A second reason, apart from the transfer of epistemic self-trust, is that beliefs of others reflect their evidence and experiences.[23] Thomas Kelly notes that we regularly treat the beliefs of others as evidence for that what they believe and that revising our beliefs in the light of what others believe is often reasonable. Especially in cases where truth cannot be discerned directly we often rely on evidence from others. Kelly argues that others might very well possess evidence that one lacks or had experiences that are unavailable. If we regard others as competent interpreters of their evidence and experiences we would expect that their beliefs reflect their evidence and experiences. For Kelly, beliefs of others are more than a reflection of how things appear from one point in physical space. They rather reflect that person's past history and experiences, the particular ways in which she responded to and interpreted these experiences, her background assumptions, and much more.[24]

Kelly's claim that relying on other people's evidence is more important for evidence or experiences that is unavailable is especially relevant for existential supernatural belief. While some of the evidence for the claim that some supernatural being exists is in principle available to everybody (e.g., standard arguments in natural theology), other evidence (e.g., evidence of revelations) is not. The number of people who had religious experiences might also be limited.

7.3.3 Reason 3: Less Surprising

A third reason for granting evidential weight to a wide occurrence of a belief p is that such a wide occurrence is surprising if p is not true. I illustrate my claim with the following thought experiment.

> X is blind from birth and lacks the ability to feel. As a result she has never seen or felt a tree.[25] When growing up she finds out that a lot of people believe that trees exist. She hears them talking about living things that shoot from the ground and have branches and leaves. She finds out that the belief in trees is not limited to a small number of people but is widely shared by a wide majority of people.

The occurrence of tree beliefs appears to be evidence for X in favor of the claim that trees exist. Given a wide occurrence of tree beliefs, a world where trees exist is more probable than a world with no trees. The fact that tree beliefs occur widely is important. Beliefs that are rare likely have a low evidential value or maybe have none at all. Belief in the existence of Sasquatch or Bigfoot is very rare. There are no statistics, but the number of Sasquatch believers probably does not exceed a few thousand. Because of its low prevalence, the occurrence of Sasquatch beliefs provides very little evidence for the claim that Sasquatch exists. Its low prevalence makes it more likely that Sasquatch beliefs result from mistakes or willful deceit. The same (probably) holds for other rare beliefs like belief in alien abductions or telekinesis.[26] The fact that they are rare makes these beliefs less likely to be true.[27]

In line with these ideas I claim that if supernatural beliefs are taken at face value, they speak in favor of supernaturalism rather than naturalism. Supernatural beliefs are more likely to occur in a world where there exists something supernatural than in a world in which there exists nothing supernatural. In a world with at least one supernatural being, it is more likely that people will form supernatural beliefs than in a world without them.

Reasoning with possible worlds is tricky when it comes to supernatural beings. For many supernatural beings, like angels or spirits, there is no problem because we can easily imagine possible worlds in which they do not exist. For others, like the God in the Christian tradition, problems arise. The God of Christianity is usually considered a necessary being.[28] Being necessary implies existing in all possible worlds. Therefore, there appears to be no possible world without supernatural beings. One notable defender of the contingency of the Christian God is Richard Swinburne. He claims that atheism is a coherent position and he thus claims that god's existence should not be considered logically necessary. He defends the claim that God is only necessary in a weaker sense, namely that "if He exists at any time He exists at all times."[29] On Swinburne's interpretation of the necessity of God, reasoning about possible worlds without supernatural beings is possible.

7.3.4 Criticisms

Contrary to what I just argued, some have argued that a wide prevalence of a belief is not evidence for the truth of that belief because other people's beliefs are merely a proxy for the evidence they rely on. John Stuart Mill famously made this point. He writes,

> It may doubtless be good advice to persons who in point of knowledge and cultivation are not entitled to think themselves competent judges of difficult questions, to bid them content themselves with holding that true which mankind generally believe . . . or that which has been believed by those who pass for the most eminent among the minds of

the past. But to a thinker the argument from other people's opinions has little weight. It is *but second-hand evidence*; and merely admonishes us to look out for and weigh the reasons on which this conviction of mankind or of wise men was founded.[30]

John Locke also argues that relying on the wide prevalence of belief in God[31] is not needed because God's existence is easily concluded to by thinking seriously.[32] Against Locke's claim, I argue that second-hand evidence is still evidence. We often rely on second-hand evidence to hold scientific or historical beliefs. Relying on second-hand evidence is needed because checking all reasons for scientific and historical belief is impossible.

Another criticism goes back to John Locke and David Hume.[33] They argue that many beliefs lack refinement by reason.[34] Hume laments the "vulgar opinions" the Japanese, Indian, and African peoples had concerning supernatural beings. Hume also points to remnants of these unrefined ideas among ancient Greek philosophers.[35] Thomas Kelly echoes this point when he writes,

> The datum [a wide prevalence of supernatural beliefs] is relatively insignificant, because the poorly informed/unenlightened/unsophisticated (etc.) are overrepresented among the theists.[36]

Locke and Hume's objections betray a commitment to what I call "epistemic elitism."[37] Adherents of epistemic elitism claim that not all people are equal in their desire for truth and epistemic powers. Locke, Mill, and Hume deny that epistemic self-trust transfers to trust of others. Instead they argue that their own epistemic abilities are superior to those of many others. Their remarks might display an old-fashioned colonial paternalism. Denying epistemic worth to beliefs of non-European peoples is no longer deemed acceptable. One could still argue that some people have better epistemic capabilities than others and hence that only their beliefs count as evidence. People with better epistemic capabilities could be people with higher IQ's or with more formal training. I agree with Zagzebski that denying trust in (many) others epistemic capabilities is uncalled for. Most people do seem able to form true beliefs about many things like trees, people, and science. There is no good reason to think that their capabilities should not be trusted when they form beliefs in or about supernatural beings. To this, Thomas Kelly adds that even if there would be evidence that most people have lower epistemic capabilities, their beliefs still provide some evidence.[38]

Another possible objection is the problem of religious diversity. This argument was originally raised against the argument from religious experience.[39] The problem of religious diversity states that religious experiences are too diverse to lend support to theism. Some people have religious experiences of the Christian God and others of Hindu gods. From this, some conclude that religious experiences give contradictory outputs and do not lend any justification. The debate whether religious diversity damages the argument from religious experience remains open.[40] One could argue in a similar way against the CGA. There appear to be many different, contradictory beliefs about what supernatural beings exist. Therefore, the wide occurrence we find would lose its evidential value. For our purposes, religious diversity seems less of a problem because supernaturalism is broader than theism. Even if people have widely diverging supernatural beliefs, the divergence will mainly be found in their substantial supernatural beliefs. Their existential supernatural beliefs will be more similar and thereby still lend support for the thesis that there exists at least something supernatural.

Zagzebski discusses another criticism.[41] A consensus could be traced back to (the testimony of) only a few people. Zagzebski acknowledges that the evidential value of a widespread belief diminishes in this case. She does claim that the evidential value of a widespread belief is still higher than that of less prevalent belief because it shows that a lot of people regard the testifier (or small group of testifiers) as trustworthy. This in turn provides a defeasible reason for trusting her (or them) too.[42] To this we can add that if a belief is transmitted over a testimonial chain, widespread trust in that chain is defeasible evidence for trusting it. For our purposes, it suffices to note that this scenario is highly unlikely.

People appear to have formed supernatural beliefs independently. Newly discovered cultures that lacked contact with other societies have been shown to hold supernatural beliefs. Being devoid from contact with other cultures, their beliefs cannot be traced back to the same testifiers as the supernatural beliefs of another culture.

Another criticism discussed by Zagzebski reverses the CGA. Atheists can claim that a large number of people do not believe in anything supernatural. This counts as evidence for the claim that nothing supernatural in fact exists. Zagzebski responds that the number of people who believe is larger than the number of people who disbelieve. Therefore, the evidence for supernaturalism is stronger than the evidence against it.[43]

7.4 Counterargument: A Naturalistic Explanation for the Wide Occurrence of Supernatural Beliefs

Some suggest that the second premise of the CGA can be defeated by scientific evidence. Thomas Kelly writes,

> Even with respect to a universally held belief, one can imagine acquiring evidence that would undermine the potential epistemic significance of the fact that it is universally held. (For example, imagine a possible world in which literally everyone believes that God exists, but in which scientists discover the following fact: because of the character of that world, belief in God has proven evolutionarily advantageous for non-truth-related reasons, and because of this all members of the species are now born with such belief hard-wired into their brains.)[44]

Kelly's claim does not make it sufficiently clear why a mechanism that shows that supernatural belief is evolutionary advantageous undermines the evidential significance[45] of a wide prevalence in supernatural beliefs. Gijsbert van den Brink makes a similar claim based on CSR theories. He argues that CSR theories can provide an alternative explanation for the origin of religious belief.[46]

In order to explain why an alternative, evolutionary explanation for religious belief undermines premise (2) the fact that an evolutionary mechanism is a naturalistic one is important. Darwinian evolution is usually seen as an account of how a diversity of traits can arise without any need for a supernatural act. Only a small minority of scholars deny this.[47] Showing that supernatural beliefs result from an evolutionary mechanism thus amounts to showing that these beliefs can be explained naturalistically. Having a mechanism of this sort shows how supernatural beliefs can arise in a naturalistic world.

The counterargument against the CGA goes as follows:

(4) CSR theories explain the wide occurrence of supernatural belief naturalistically.
(5) CSR theories offer the best explanation of a wide occurrence of supernatural belief.
(6) If a wide occurrence of supernatural belief is best explained naturalistically, a wide occurrence of supernatural belief is as probable under naturalism as it is under supernaturalism.
(7) Therefore, a wide occurrence of supernatural belief is as probable under naturalism as it is under supernaturalism.

Conclusion (7) denies the conclusion of the CGA. Premise (4) states that CSR theories do not refer to anything supernatural to explain the wide occurrence of supernatural beliefs. The premise does not say that CSR theories (or scientific theories in general) *should not* refer to anything supernatural.[48] It merely states a factual claim.

Premise (4) can be cashed out in at least two ways; one in which CSR theories explain

(i) why there is a *wide* occurrence of supernatural belief and
(ii) why supernatural belief is formed.

To explain (i), adaptationist CSR theories are most suited (see Section 2.2). By showing that supernatural belief is or was adaptive, theories can explain why supernatural belief was transmitted and spread widely across the human population. The adaptationist theory need not explain how supernatural belief is formed in individual subjects. It suffices to argue that some individuals formed supernatural beliefs and that these individuals outcompeted others without supernatural beliefs. For example, if the BSPT is true, it can show that belief in a morally concerned, punishing or rewarding God with access to people's thoughts spread throughout the human population because the belief benefited human cooperation.[49] The explanation is naturalistic because the theory argues that the *wide* occurrence of supernatural beliefs is due to natural causes, namely, the mechanisms of natural selection.

To explain (ii), cognitive bias theories are better suited. We saw that adaptationist CSR theories do not provide details about how supernatural belief is formed in individuals. An adaptationist theory could argue that supernatural belief was randomly thrown up and was retained because of its adaptive value. An explanation in these terms, however, does not explain why a majority of individuals today form supernatural beliefs. Bias CSR theories can explain this. For example, if the theory of HADD is true, individuals form supernatural beliefs because of the hyperactive operations of their agency detection systems (see Section 2.3.5). The explanation must, however, take the input into account. It is therefore only naturalistic if supernatural beliefs are the result of a misattribution. The HADD can only naturalistically explain why individuals form supernatural beliefs if it can show that individuals form supernatural beliefs after wrongfully processing natural input. We saw in Section 5.6 in Chapter 5 that bias CSR theories do not present a convincing case for this claim. Until they do, cognitive bias theories do not support premise (4).

Having established that adaptationist CSR theories, if true, can naturalistically explain a *wide* occurrence of supernatural belief does not yet support the counterargument. The explanation needs to be *better* than rivaling (supernatural) explanations. Examples of rivaling supernatural explanations can come in two variants. The first rejects the naturalistic explanations and argue that the wide occurrence of supernatural belief is due to some supernatural act. Daniel Lim calls explanations of this kinds "folk theism."[50] Lim's example is how most (Christian) believers explain Moses supernatural encounter on Mount Horeb. Believers who take the biblical account of the encounter at face value will claim that a supernatural being literally spoke to Moses. For Moses himself, a supernatural act seems to be the *direct* cause of his supernatural belief.[51] Lim's account can also be applied to supernatural beliefs that are not formed after an intense religious experience. A folk theistic explanation for religious beliefs could state that God makes Himself known during liturgy or prayer and the subject subsequently forms a supernatural belief or that humans unconsciously pick up signs of God's activity.

Like cognitive bias explanations, folk theistic explanations can explain how religious beliefs are formed in individuals. Like adaptationist theories, they can also explain why supernatural belief occurs *widely*. Defenders can add that supernatural acts occur widely and lead to a wide occurrence of supernatural belief. The question is which explanation is better, the explanation based on adaptationist CSR theories or the folk theistic explanation. One could argue that folk theistic explanations are not open to rigid empirical corroboration whereas CSR-based explanations are. Adaptationist CSR theories can be tested by means of computer simulation or by studying whether supernatural belief correlates with better cooperation. Folk theistic explanations rely mainly on testimonial support.

Another supernaturalistic explanation is possible. One could accept the causal story adaptationist CSR theories provide and claim that supernatural belief spread because of its adaptive value. One could then add that the adaptive value is not the only cause of the wide occurrence of supernatural belief. God or another supernatural being could have set up the initial conditions for human evolution in such a way that supernatural beliefs would be adaptive. In this way, God is the ultimate cause of the way human evolution took shape.[52] On this explanation, a supernatural being is the *indirect* cause of the wide occurrence of supernatural belief. This indirect supernaturalistic explanation resembles a common stance toward CSR, although the response is usually directed at bias CSR theories.[53]

From the point of view of the CGA, the indirect supernaturalistic explanation does not seem better than the naturalistic CSR-based explanation. The supernaturalistic explanation adds a supernatural being at a deeper level of explanation. Moving to a deeper level is not needed to explain our explanandum, that is, the wide occurrence of supernatural belief. Because of this, the indirect supernaturalistic explanation is less parsimonious. The principle of parsimony states that theories should not postulate more kinds of entities than required.[54] The principle is not without its critics[55] but is widely accepted. Therefore, the indirect supernaturalistic explanation also does not seem better than the naturalistic, CSR-based explanation.

The conclusion (7) follows from premises (4), (5), and (6). It denies the second premise of my version of the CGA. Below, I look closer at premise (6) and assess whether the naturalistic explanation drawn from CSR theories makes a wide occurrence of supernatural belief as probable under naturalism as under supernaturalism. I will return to the three reasons in support of premise (2) and investigate whether they are still good reasons.

7.5 Criticizing the Counterargument

7.5.1 Do They Still Reflect People's Experiences and Evidence?

Kelly argues that a wide occurrence of supernatural belief is evidence for supernaturalism because the wide occurrence reflects individual experiences and evidence. I argued above that adaptationist CSR theories are the best candidates to explain the wide occurrence. I noted in Chapter 2 that adaptationist CSR theories do not aim to explain religious experiences. They might be wedded to an explanation for religious experiences,[56] but by themselves they have little bearing on supernatural beliefs formed after religious experiences.

Adaptationist CSR theories also do not make it doubtful that a wide occurrence of supernatural belief (partly) reflects individual's evidence. Individuals can still come to hold supernatural beliefs by looking at the evidence and their assessment is not affected by an adaptationist CSR theory. Their assessment of evidence might be hampered by a cognitive mechanism that goes astray. In their book *A Natural History of Natural Religion*, Helen De Cruz and Johan De Smedt suggest that a number of arguments recruit the same cognitive mechanisms like "ordinary" religious cognition does. They discuss the teleological argument (also known as the design argument), cosmological argument, moral argument, argument from beauty, and the argument from religious experience. For each of these arguments they discuss how cognitive mechanisms laid bare by CSR theories might explain why people find them convincing (and in some cases why some people find them unconvincing). For example, they suggest that the teleological bias (see Section 2.3.4) could explain why people find the teleological argument convincing.[57] De Cruz and De Smedt are careful to draw conclusions about the evidential value of their claim. Their claim does suggest that many people do not find arguments in natural theology convincing because of the force of the arguments but rather because of the (unconscious) operations of some cognitive bias. If the suggestion of De Cruz and De Smedt is true, a bias explanation could also diminish the evidential value of supernatural beliefs based on evidence. An argument for this claim, however, relies on the success of a misattribution argument (see Section 5.6).

7.5.2 Not Improbable Under Naturalism Anymore?

A different way naturalistic explanation reduces the evidential value of supernatural beliefs is by showing that supernatural beliefs are not surprising in a naturalistic world. We noted that on naturalism the occurrence of supernatural beliefs is something strange, something that is not to be expected since there are no supernatural beings. If there is a mechanism that naturalistically brings about supernatural beliefs this is no longer the case. The existence of such a mechanism makes the occurrence of supernatural beliefs even likely.

Our tree analogy is again helpful here. In a world without trees, a wide occurrence of tree beliefs is highly improbable. If there is a mechanism that produces tree beliefs without any need for trees, tree beliefs are no longer improbable, but even likely. Similarly, a naturalistic mechanism for supernatural belief can turn supernatural beliefs from a surprising fact to an unsurprising fact for naturalism.

7.5.3 Undermines Trust?

Another reason that appears to be somewhat affected is trust. If an adaptationist CSR theory is true, people do not hold supernatural beliefs because they are true but because they are evolutionary beneficial. We saw in Section 5.4.2 in Chapter 5 that adaptive value and being sensitive to truth can be connected via a Milvian Bridge. If having true supernatural beliefs increase the chances of human survival, religious cognitive faculties are not unreliable and can be trusted. I argued that a Milvian Bridge is indeed available for supernatural beliefs insofar as they yield successful engagement with God or another supernatural being and a life of sanctity.

While my response can uphold the reliability of an individual's belief-forming faculties, there might be a problem if we apply it to the whole human population. Alston notes that his account of sanctity is somewhat elitist. Not all religious believers spend the time and effort to cultivate their engagement with God in a way that produces more sanctity. How many people do is hard to assess. It is, however, likely that many religious believers do not. Not only do many lack the time to do so, many probably also do not see the value or worth of doing so. Caution is therefore warranted against trusting that the majority of religious believers make the effort of cultivating their religious practices. As a result, trust appears to be somewhat undermined.

7.6 Conclusion

In this chapter I discussed the CGA and how CSR theories can affect it. I argued that adaptationist CSR theories can undermine the argument to some extent. By affecting trust and by showing that supernatural beliefs are not improbable on naturalism, an adaptationist CSR theory can harm the evidential value of a wide occurrence of supernatural beliefs. Its evidential value is, however, not completely defused and the wide occurrence could still reflect people's experiences and evidence. Therefore, it is not clear how much the evidential value is harmed and how much more probable naturalism becomes. Overall, the CGA does not appear to be fully refuted.

Conclusion

I started off with the question whether CSR theories can serve a debunking argument against religious belief. The answer leans strongly toward "no." I argued that CSR theories are not incompatible with the content of religious beliefs; that CSR theories do not show that supernatural beliefs are unreliably formed; that CSR theories do not undo the evidential value of religious experiences; and that CSR theories have only limited implications on the evidential status of a wide occurrence of supernatural beliefs.

My answer "no" needs to be qualified. I did not discuss all CSR theories. Though I believe I covered the most influential theories in CSR in Chapters 2 and 3, other theories are around and new, better theories will very likely be proposed in the future. Some of my arguments can be applied to arguments that rely on other theories as well. The discussion in Chapter 3 shows that a theory will have to make claims that are significantly different than "religious beliefs are caused by cognitive mechanisms and/or evolutionary pressures," "religious beliefs arise intuitively," or "religious rituals serve an evolutionary function" in order to make some kind of incompatibility argument plausible. My conclusion in Chapter 4 (that arguments that argue for unreliability by showing that belief-forming faculties responsible for supernatural belief evolved or produce many false beliefs) will also apply to other theories.

A second reason why my "no" needs to be qualified is that there might be other kinds of arguments. I have not come across such other arguments. Furthermore it is hard to see how arguments can take a different route than arguing for incompatibility, unreliability, or a naturalistic explanation to conclude to an epistemic deficiency.

Nowhere in this thesis did I argue that an argument based on CSR theories could never conclude to a serious epistemic deficit of religious or supernatural beliefs. An incompatibility argument will likely be the most difficult. It is hard to see what claim CSR theories can make that will conflict with a religious truth claim that is widely held. They might make claims that conflict with religious claims that are not commonly held. For example, future research in CSR could show that the operations of cognitive mechanisms responsible for religious belief cannot be altered. This could conflict with a claim held in some new age religions that people can evolve into a new state of mind, a state where they are only open to true (religious) knowledge. Since the prevalence of belief in such a claim is quite rare, such an argument will be quite trivial.

New developments in CSR can change the conclusions of the most straightforward arguments. The most promising road for an unreliability argument is probably a misattribution argument. If CSR theories were to convincingly show that supernatural belief results from mistakes or false positives in a non-question-begging way, a strong case can be made that supernatural beliefs suffer from a serious epistemic deficit. CSR theories of religious experiences of broader scope with a clear naturalistic causal explanation could also undo the evidential value of religious experiences. Successful arguments for unreliability and against the evidential value of religious experiences could also be more successful in refuting the CGA.

Whether future arguments will be successful is thus largely dependent on the quality of future CSR theories or other explanations of religious phenomena. As I noted, it is hard to assess the future of CSR. Some CSR theories have been heavily criticized. No theory has gained the support of most theorists and empirical support is often lacking. Future debunking arguments against religious belief of any kind will have to be cautious in relying too heavily on CSR theories. They should also pay close attention to what CSR theorists claim and how well their claims are supported.

Notes

Introduction

1. For example, Trivers (1971) and Greene (2014).
2. Famous arguments against morality were defended by Michael Ruse and Edwar O. Wilson (1986), Sharon Street (2006) and Richard Joyce (2007).
3. Joyce (2007), Ruse and Wilson (1986) and Street (2006).
4. For example, Cuneo and Shafer-Landau (2014), and FitzPatrick (2015).
5. For example, Kyriacou (2017).
6. Often debunking arguments refer to Guy Kahane's general schema for evolutionary debunking arguments (Kahane 2011). Kahane's schema, however, only applies to *evolutionary* debunking arguments.
7. Libet (1985).
8. Wegner (2002).
9. For example, Asma (2017).
10. Plantinga (2011).
11. De Cruz et al. (2011).
12. James (1902: Lecture 1).
13. Freud (1961).
14. We should note here that neither James's or Freud's main goal was presenting or defending a debunking argument against religious belief.
15. David Leech and Aku Visala list a number of passages from cognitive scientists that suggest debunking claims (Leech and Visala 2011b). Michael Murray presents self-constructed arguments that preempt challenges (Murray 2008).
16. For a more complete overview of recent debunking arguments against religious belief, see Van Eyghen, Peels, and Van den Brink (2018).

Chapter 1

1. Examples are John Wilkins and Paul Griffiths (2013), Michael Murray (2008), James Jones (2016), David Leech and Aku Visala (2011a) and Robert Nola (2013).

2   Kelly Clark, for example, explicitly discusses belief in God, both in solo work and in a paper with Justin Barrett (2010) (Clark 2010). Liz Goodnick's argument, see section 5.4.2, is also aimed at belief in God (2016). Joshua Thurow uses the term belief in "a god of some kind" (Thurow 2013: 77). Justin Barrett uses the term "belief in gods" (2007: 57).
3   In a paper with Dani Rabinowitz, Kelly Clark uses "theistic belief" (2011). Matthew Braddock uses the term "theistic beliefs" and "god-beliefs" interchangeably (2016).
4   Jonathan Jong and Aku Visala refer to "theism" (2014).
5   Jong, Kavanagh, and Visala (2015: 244).
6   See (Van Inwagen 2009: 129).
7   For example, Daniel Dubuisson writes, "Christianity, in a very specific historical context, invented the idea . . . of religion. Moreover, several intrinsic characteristics that defined its content were progressively associated with this 'western construction of religion'" (2007: 787).
8   One can think here of Paul Tillich's definition of religion as "ultimate concern" (1953), and see that it easily applies to political ideologies or sports.
9   For examples, beliefs about how an offering to spirits ought to be performed depend on the belief that spirits "like" the offerings or "need" the offerings.
10 See Wittgenstein (1958).
11 See Saler (1999).
12 There is considerable debate over what the tern "supervenience" amounts to. For a discussion of varieties of supervenience, see McLaughlin and Bennett (2005). In its most generic form something supervenes on something else if there can be no changes in the supervening thing without changes in the thing it supervenes upon.
13 See Ladyman (2011).
14 Here, I use a common-sense definition of "being" where beings are living beings. This excludes nonphysical things like social institutions or numbers, which naturalists tend to allow in their ontologies.
15 Sometimes supernatural beings are believed to exist in space and time. The Christian God is sometimes claimed to exist in space and time after creation. For a discussion, see Ganssle (2001) and Craig (2001). Christians also believe that God was incarnate in Jesus in space and time.
16 I previously used these three conditions to define supernaturalism (Van Eyghen 2018b).

17 See Ferrari (2014: 95–97)
18 Richard Kieckheffer distinguish these experiences of union with "habitual union" where a subject experiences a lasting consciousness of God during daily activities. Kieckheffer also distinguishes a third kind of union which combines both kinds (1978).
19 Theresa of Avila was a Carmelite nun at the time of her experiences so she likely already believed in God. Her experiences probably did reinforce her belief.
20 See Mitchel (1993: 26).
21 See Davis (1993: 107).
22 The argument from religious experiences roughly states that religious experiences can lend justification for belief in the existence of God or that religious experiences make theism more probable than atheism (see also chapter 6).
23 See Kwan (2009: 500).
24 See Kwan (2009: 500).

Chapter 2

1 For example, Asprem (2017).
2 For example, Hayes and Timalsina (2017).
3 Lawson and McCauley (1990).
4 Luhrmann (2012).
5 Jong, Kavanagh, and Visala (2015: 250).
6 Personal conversations with Robert McCauley, Michiel van Elk, and Bastiaan Ruitjens (all theorists in the field) convinced me that Jong, Kavanagh, and Visala's claim is somewhat overstated.
7 Atran (2002: 4).
8 Defenders of BSPT seem to argue that supernatural beliefs were both evolutionarily beneficial in the past and still are today. BGT (see next section) puts the evolutionary advantage solely in the past, that is, around the time of the emergence of large societies.
9 The theory also goes by different names. Dominic Johnson and Jesse Bering call it supernatural punishment (Johnson and Bering 2009). Like

Watts et al. (2015), I use the term broad supernatural punishment because it allows a better distinction between the BSPT and the BGT (see below) that also puts a lot of emphasis on supernatural punishment.
10 Bering and Johnson (2005: 128–30).
11 Bering and Johnson (2005: 131).
12 Bering and Johnson (2005: 120).
13 Bering and Johnson (2005).
14 One might argue that different cultures appear to value different desires and goals. Johnson and Bering acknowledge that what amounts to important information can vary from culture to culture but cite evidence that children are already able to differentiate moral imperatives from social conventions. Breaching social conventions seems to be associated with more tolerance than the breaching of moral imperatives. They thereby claim that while the content of strategic information can vary, the idea that there is a distinct set of information of this sort exists cross-culturally. I lack the background to assess the evidence cited by Johnson and Bering. They cite one book about moral development (Turiel 2002), one review article about research on shame (Gilbert 1998) and one about self-conscious emotions (Tangney 2001). They do not direct their readers in greater detail toward evidence for the claim that children are able to differentiate moral imperatives from social conventions.
15 Bering and Johnson (2005: 126–27).
16 Bering and Johnson (2005: 130).
17 Bering and Johnson (2005).
18 Shariff and Norenzayan (2011).
19 Bering and Johnson (2005: 131–33).
20 One could object that God concepts like those in the Hebrew Bible arrive on the scene much later and are (heavily) affected by cultural evolution and not biological evolution. There is, however, also evidence for god concepts that foster tribalism in earlier times. For example, in Homer's *Iliad* (usually dated in the eighth century BC) Greek gods take sides in the Trojan War and encourage the struggle between both sides. While we know little about ancient Greek religion, the *Iliad* signals that ancient Greeks did believe that some supernatural beings sometimes favored tribalism.
21 DeBono, Shariff, and Muraven (2012).

22 Mckay and Whitehouse (2014).
23 Shariff (2015: 113).
24 See, for example, Saroglou (2012).
25 For example, Shariff et al. write, "*Some* gods can even read people's thoughts" (Shariff, Norenzayan, and Henrich 2009: 124 emphasis added). We noted when discussing BSPT that Shariff was critical of an unambiguous connection between supernatural beliefs and morality. Yet he also defends BGT.
26 Shariff, Norenzayan, and Henrich (2009).
27 Shariff, Norenzayan, and Henrich (2009: 126–27).
28 Shariff, Norenzayan, and Henrich (2009).
29 Roes and Raymond (2003: 130).
30 Bering, Piazza, and Ingram (2011).
31 Randolph-Seng and Nielsen (2007) and Mazar, Amir, and Ariely (2008).
32 Gervais and Norenzayan (2012a).
33 Norenzayan (2013).
34 Malhotra (2008).
35 Edelman (2009).
36 Norenzayan (2013).
37 Norenzayan (2013: 46).
38 Baumard and Boyer (2013: 272).
39 Whitehouse et al. (2019).
40 Beheim et al. (2019).
41 Slone and Slyke (2015a).
42 Slone and Slyke (2015b: 2).
43 "Useless" should be read as evolutionary wasteful. These traits and behaviors are not necessarily considered useless by the individual who displays them. From an evolutionary point of view they serve no immediate use and seem a waste of resources.
44 Slone and Van Slyke (2015b) give the example of a peacock's tail. The tail is costly and serves no immediate evolutionary purpose. Furthermore, the tail slows the peacock down, making it more vulnerable to predators. Yet having the tail signals that a male peacock has so many resources that it can afford to waste some of it on the tail.
45 Slone and Slyke (2015b: 3).
46 Bulbulia et al. (2015).

47 McCullough and Willoughby (2009).
48 Bulbulia et al. refer to John Shaver's "The Behavioral Ecology of Fijian Religion." This is John Shaver's PHD thesis and it has not been published (as far as I know). Therefore, I was unable to find it. However, I found an article that Shaver wrote in collaboration with Richard Sosis where he makes a similar claim like the one cited by Bulbulia et al.
49 Shaver and Sosis (2014).
50 Bulbulia et al. (2015: 33)
51 Martinez and Lienard (2015).
52 Palmer and Begley (2015).
53 Claims of this sort go back to medieval philosophers like Thomas Aquinas and early modern thinkers like René Descartes.
54 For example, McCauley (2015) and Bogen (2013).
55 For example, Gopnik, Meltzoff, and Kuhl (1999) and Carruthers (1996).
56 Claire White illustrates this when she writes, "What most distinguishes CSR from other approaches to the study of religion is the active role attributed to human cognition in the formation and transmission of religious ideas" (2017: 12).
57 For example, Jespen Sorensen writes, "Failure to recognize the importance of underlying cognitive processing has lead [sic] to an over- emphasis on the 'exotic' nature of religion" (2005: 471). Pascal Boyer writes,"Belief in religion activates mental systems involved in a whole variety of non-religious domains" (2004: 2). Dan Sperber and Lawrence Hirschfeld write, "Religious beliefs can be seen as parasitical on domain- specific competencies that they both exploit and challenge" (1999: cxx).
58 See Barrett (2004a), McCauley (2011), and Bloom (2007).
59 An example of this confusion is found in Peter van Inwagen's paper (2009). When discussing Paul Bloom's theory of the dualist bias, he objects that he himself does not have the belief in mind-body dualism that is predicted by the theory. While he might not have the reflective belief in mind-body dualism, Van Inwagen might have an intuitive belief of this sort. This is compatible with Bloom's theory.
60 This view was popularized by Daniel Kahnemann (2012).
61 Sperber (1997: 68).
62 Sperber (1997).
63 Sperber (1997: 70–71).

64 Barrett uses the term "nonreflective beliefs."
65 Barrett (2004b: 12–13).
66 Barrett (2004b: 14–15).
67 Boyer (2002: 3).
68 Boyer (2002: 60).
69 Boyer (2002: 66)
70 One notable exception is Justin Barrett. He argues that reflective supernatural beliefs can be very diverse but that the diversity is rather superficial. He did a number of experiments where he asked religious believers a number of questions about their beliefs. Under normal circumstances, they give what Barrett calls "theological correct answers," that is, answers that match the doctrine of the religion they adhere to. When put under time pressure, they tend to give "theologically incorrect" answers, that is, answers more in line with intuitive beliefs (Barrett 1998, 1999). Barrett thus suggests that reflective beliefs are a surface phenomenon and what really drives people's (religious) behavior are intuitive beliefs.
71 There is a third option. Some authors argued that supernatural beliefs could have served no adaptive use for a good part of human evolutionary history but later did. The approach is sometimes called "exaptionist" (e.g. Richerson and Newson 2008). I will not discuss this at length because it is not important for the arguments I discuss in the next chapters.
72 The term is inspired by Kelly Clark and Justin Barrett's use of the term "preparedness account" (2010: 182).
73 Kelemen (2004).
74 Kelemen (1999).
75 Kelemen (1999).
76 Kelemen (2003). Her findings were also replicated among British children to test for the claim that a teleological bias is merely a reflection of the religious exceptionalism of the United States (Kelemen 2003).
77 Evans (2000).
78 Kelemen and rossett (2009).
79 Casler and Kelemen (2008).
80 Bloom (2007).
81 Bloom (2004).
82 Lindeman, Svedholm-Häkkinen, and Lipsanen (2015: 65).

83 Lindeman, Svedholm-Häkkinen, and Lipsanen (2015: 65).
84 See, for example, Boyer (2002: 66–75).
85 Lindeman, Svedholm-Häkkinen, and Lipsanen (2015: 65).
86 Bering and Bjorklund (2004).
87 The idea of simulation roughly means that people imagine themselves in a particular mental state. According to some this is how people form beliefs about other's mental states.
88 Bering (2002b).
89 Hodge, Sousa, and White (unpublished).
90 Nichols (2007).
91 Bek and Lock (2011).
92 Hodge (2016).
93 Lane et al. (2016)
94 Hodge, Sousa, and White (unpublished).
95 I cannot go into detail much what makes up personal identity. Following the authors discussed above, it mainly consists of a person's emotional and epistemic states.
96 Guthrie (2007: 37).
97 Barrett (2004b: 31).
98 Barrett (2004b: 31).
99 Barrett (2004b).
100 Barrett (2004b: 33).
101 Barrett (2004b: 33).
102 Elsewhere Barrett argued that some religious traditions provide these reflective defenses (see Barrett and Church 2013).
103 Barrett (2004b: 33).
104 Barrett (2004b: 33).
105 Barrett (2004b: 34).
106 Barrett (2004b).
107 Gray and Wegner (2011: 109–10).
108 Gray and Wegner (2011: 112–13).
109 Gray and Wegner (2010: 9).
110 The theologically schooled reader will recognize this view as the impassibility of God. Apart from the study, Gray and Wegner do not provide much evidence why most common believers would believe in God's impassibility. Nonetheless, many CSR theorists argue that many

common believers hold anthropomorphic beliefs about God (Slone, 2004). If this is the case, belief in God's impassibility is probably not as widespread as Gray and Wegner claim it to be.
111 Gray and Wegner (2011).
112 Gray, Gray, and Wegner (2007).
113 Gray and Wegner (2010).
114 Gray and Wegner (2011).
115 Gray and Wegner (2010).
116 Bering (2002a: 3).
117 Bering (2002a: 3).
118 Bering (2002a: 4).
119 Bering (2002a: 4).
120 Bering (2002a).
121 Bering (2002a).
122 Bering (2002a: 12).
123 Bering (2002a: 10).
124 Boyer (2002).
125 Boyer (2002: 37).
126 Boyer uses the terms "gods" and "spirits."
127 I have not discussed Boyer's views when discussing BSPT because Bering and Johnson's defense is more elaborate.

Chapter 3

1. Terence Cuneo offers an account of how ritual behavior is aimed at engaging with God (2014).
2. Ianneconne (1992).
3. Sosis and Bressler (2003) Sosis (2005) Bulbulia and Sosis (2011) and Sosis and Kiper (2014).
4. For example, Atran (2002), Atran and Henrich (2010), and Irons (2001).
5. Sosis (2005).
6. Sosis (2000).
7. Ruffle and Sosis (2005).
8. Xygalatas et al. (2013).

9 Murray and Moore (2009: 226).
10 Bulbulia and Sosis (2011).
11 Murray and Moore (2009).
12 Murray and Moore (2009).
13 Whitehouse and Lanman (2014).
14 Elsewhere, the terms "local fusion" and "extended fusion" are used with "extended fusion" corresponding to "social identification" and "local fusion" to "identity fusion" (cf. Swann et al. 2012).
15 Whitehouse et al. (2013).
16 Whitehouse et al. (2013: 285). Whitehouse borrowed the term "imagined communities" from Benedict Anderson (2004).
17 Whitehouse et al. (2013: 282).
18 Whitehouse et al. (2013).
19 Whitehouse et al. (2013).
20 Whitehouse et al. (2013).
21 Whitehouse et al. (2013).
22 Whitehouse et al. (2014).
23 Cohen, Mundry, and Kirschner (2014).
24 Boyer and Liénard (2006).
25 Boyer and Liénard (2006: 4).
26 Boyer and Liénard add that the HPC responds to threats that were important in the evolutionary history of mankind. For this reason, the HPC would be triggered more easily by predators than by urban traffic (2006: 8).
27 Boyer and Liénard (2006).
28 Boyer and Liénard (2006).
29 Beauregard and Paquette (2006).
30 Azari et al. (2001).
31 The discussion on Michael Persinger and his God Helmet is drawn from my earlier paper "*Spirit Beliefs Debunked*" (Van Eyghen 2018c).
32 Persinger (1985).
33 Booth and Persinger (2009).
34 A Swedish team led by Pehr Granqvist tried to replicate the experiment but concluded that the higher prevalence in reports of a sensed presence were due to suggestion (Granqvist et al. 2005). Persinger and his team

responded that the methodology in the replication was significantly different than in the original setup (Persinger and Koren 2005).
35   The discussion of predictive coding below is an abbreviated version of my discussion in (Van Eyghen 2018a).
36   My discussion of PC mainly relies on Andy Clark's overview of the theory (Clark 2013). His theory has a broader scope than perceptual experience. Since the theory I discuss in the third section focuses on perceptual experiences, I limit the discussion to those experiences in this section.
37   Hawkins and Blakeslee (2004: 158).
38   Andy Clark calls this "the brain explaining away the sensory signals" (2013).
39   Friston (2010).
40   Andersen refers to Boyer (2002), who argues that subjects easily remember and transmit concepts that are minimally counterintuitive, and to Whitehouse (Whitehouse 2004), who argues that participation in religious rituals has a profound effect on the transmission of religious beliefs.
41   Andersen got the example from Tanya Luhrmann's work (2012). Luhrmann did fieldwork in a Pentecostal church and noted that people were taught to identify thoughts as infused by God. She argues at length that the identification process requires time and instruction by experts.
42   Xygalatas discussed the effects of extreme Hindu rituals in Mauritius on people's moral behavior
      (Xygalatas et al. 2013)
43   Andersen (2017).
44   Van Elk and Aleman (2017).

Chapter 4

1   Helen De Cruz did defend a more specific incompatibility argument (see below).
2   Bering writes, "After first examining the mechanics of belief, we'll eventually explore . . . the possibility that God (and others like him) evolved in human minds as an 'adaptive illusion'" (Bering 2012: 7).

3   Dawkins (2007: 184–86).
4   Popular writers or speakers who suggest a similar claim are Michael Shermer (2012) and Andy Thomson (2009). Both authors' arguments are, however, hard to pin down.
5   Dennett (2006: 120).
6   Dennett (2006: 121). His remarks can also be interpreted as an unreliability claim (see Chapter 5).
7   "Going awry" can also be interpreted as an unreliability claim (see Chapter 5).
8   Bloom (2005) quoted by Barrett (2007: 60).
9   See Atran (2002).
10 Leech and Visala (2011b).
11 Atran (2002: 95) quoted by Leech and Visala (2011b: 51).
12 Boyer (2002: 68) quoted by Leech and Visala (2011b: 51–52).
13 Boyer (2003: 119, emphasis added) quoted by Leech and Visala (2011b: 52).
14 Jong (2012: 525).
15 Leech and Visala (2011a: 301).
16 It is worth noting that some CSR theorists are religious believers themselves. Justin Barrett is an evangelical Christian and Jonathan Jong is a minister in the Church of England.
17 This formulation is drawn from Van Eyghen (2016: 968). The rest of this section is an expanded version of what I wrote in this paper.
18 To my knowledge, no philosopher of science has criticized premise 1 as I stated it. Some have criticized the claim that scientific theories make truth claims but made no explicit claim about whether CSR theories do. Since CSR theories are scientific theories, their criticism applies to them too.
19 A famous defender is Bas van Fraassen (1980).
20 For example, we saw how Jonathan Jong, Christopher Kavanagh, and Aku Visala raised doubts about the empirical backing of CSR theories (Jong, Kavanagh, and Visala 2015)
21 (Phillips 1976). Since his work predates the first CSR theories, Philips did not have CSR theories in mind when making his claim.
22 In a recent survey among academic philosophers 75.1 percent agreed with scientific realism (Bourget and Chalmers 2013: 15). No data for philosophy of religion are available to my knowledge.

23 I omitted a possible conflict between a religious claim that God wants all people to know him and a scientific claim that some individuals are more susceptible to religious ideas than others. Some research suggests gender differences in religious beliefs and differences along the autism spectrum (e.g., Gervais and Norenzayan 2012b). I omitted this potential conflict because the theories that (allegedly) support the scientific claim have not developed as far as the theories I discussed in Chapter 2.

24 For example, the first conflict we discuss below targets the proposition that people get their religious beliefs from a supernatural cause. If the incompatibility argument against this proposition is sound, it might be more damaging for new age traditions that emphasize the importance of direct contact with God or gods.

25 Van den Brink (2018: chapter 9). A similar claim is suggested by Jonathan Jong (Jong 2012: 526).

26 De Cruz adds that CSR theories do not render this metaphysically impossible. She writes, "While the etiology of RRPs [ritual religious practices] does not rule out that humans would connect with God through rituals, the etiological accounts outlined here (which are the main CSR accounts about rituals on offer) make this doubtful. They give us good independent reason to think that the practice is not successful in engaging God" (De Cruz 2018: 21).

27 De Cruz also refers to the hazard precaution model Boyer and Liénard (2006). Her arguments are mostly drawn from the etiology laid out in the CST.

28 De Cruz (2018).

29 De Cruz (2018: 21).

30 De Cruz (2018).

31 See Gervais (2013).

32 See Hall, Matz, and Wood (2010).

33 See Atran (2002).

34 De Cruz (2018: 13).

35 Dundas (2004).

36 See, for example, Priest and Berto (2013). The term "Di-aletheism" is derived from the Greek term for double truth.

37 Priest and Berto write, "That dialetheism *challenges* the LNC [Law of Noncontradiction] needs qualification, since the LNC is accepted as

a general logical law in the mainstream versions of the theory. But a dialetheist manifests her dialetheism in accepting, together with the LNC, sentences that are inconsistent with it, that is, true sentences whose negations are true: dialetheias" (Priest and Berto 2013).

38 Van den Brink (2018: chapter 9). Although I believe his response is aimed more against the claim that the CSR causes of religious belief conflict with religious causes (see below).
39 For example, Van Inwagen (2009).
40 Van den Brink (2018: chapter 9).
41 Van Inwagen (2009).
42 Van Inwagen (2009: 134–35).
43 Van Inwagen (2009: 135).
44 They sometimes claim that religious belief is caused by divine revelation. I discuss the potential conflict between CSR claims and revelation below.
45 Theories on religious rituals and religious experiences are not important here because they do not discuss causes of religious beliefs. Having a religious experience can be regarded as a cause of religious beliefs. I will, however, discuss arguments against religious experiences separately in Chapter 6.
46 It is worth noting that the conflict will probably only arise with the BSPT and the ART. The BGT only aims to explain bigger (creating) gods and the CST explains the role of rituals.
47 Plantinga (2000). Plantinga does not take a firm stance on whether the *sensus divinitatis* actually exists in his book. He argues that if God exists he likely endowed people with a sensus divinitatis, if he doesn't exist he obviously did not. Plantinga's other work (see, for example, Plantinga 1986) makes it abundantly clear that he claims that the first part of the conditional is true. We can thus conclude that he believes that the sensus divinitatis exists.
48 Clark and Barrett (2010). When Clark and Barrett use the expression "Hard to shake," they mean to say that religious beliefs often maintain a hold on people even if they do not explicitly avow them. This feature is apparent when self-proclaimed atheists pray during times of great distress or at important moments in their lives.
49 Clark and Barrett (2010: 184).
50 This is of course possible in hybrid theories.

51 For example, Herman Philipse raises some worries about the sensus divinitatis (Philipse 2012). Erik Baldwin and Michael Thume argue that Reformed Epistemology (the broader framework wherein Plantinga's idea of the sensus divinitatis features) has problems coping with religious pluralism (Baldwin and Thune 2008). Jeroen de Ridder (in collaboration with Mathanja Berger) argues that the problems to which all three authors point are not problems or that they can be overcome (de Ridder and Berger 2013; de Ridder 732011). Whether the problems with the *sensus divinitatis* can be overcome or not, it is clear that opting for Clark and Barrett's response is a more difficult route than opting for the first response where supernatural beings make use of cognitive mechanisms.
52 Ross (1998: 13).
53 De Ridder and van Woudenberg (2014). De Ridder and van Woudenberg add that this view on general revelation draws from the Reformed tradition. I believe that it applies to many other Christian traditions as well.
54 See, for example, Barth (1957: Volume I.1).
55 The problem of evil has a long history. It argues that the presence of (massive) evil in the world is hard to reconcile with the existence of an omnibenevolent, all-powerful being.
56 For example, Bertrand Russell sees human fear as an element that supports naturalism over theism when he writes, "Man's origin, his hopes and fears, his loves and beliefs, are but the outcome of accidental co-locations of atoms" (Russell 1957: 107) quoted by (Howard-Snyder 1996: 143). Daniel Howard-Snyder also discusses fear in the context of the problem of evil: "There is fear that I'll once more make an ass of myself in an upcoming sticky situation, embarrassment at some foolish or ill-conceived thing I've said, pique or disappointment" (Howard-Snyder 1996: 255).
57 For example, Rowe (1979).
58 Influential responses are John Hick's "soul-making defense" (1974) and Alvin Plantinga's "free will defense" (1975).
59 Similarly, on the ART, someone who performs rituals signals that she is a reliable partner. De Cruz, however, does not mention this theory.
60 Whitehouse et al. (2013).
61 Boudry (2018).

62 See Exod. 34:22 "Celebrate the Festival of Weeks with the firstfruits of the wheat harvest, and the Festival of Ingathering at the turn of the year" (NIV). One can debate whether the harvest festival had a religious significance. It certainly was not an occasion for remembering the exodus. The reason why people took part in the festival thus altered and this suffices for my point.

63 See Lev. 23:42-43: "Live in temporary shelters for seven days: All native-born Israelites are to live in such shelters so your descendants will know that I had the Israelites live in temporary shelters when I brought them out of Egypt. I am the Lord your God" (NIV).

64 A Christian could refer to Mt. 6:5-6: "And when you pray, you must not be like the hypocrites. For they love to stand and pray in the synagogues and at the street corners, that they may be seen by others. Truly, I say to you, they have received their reward. 6 But when you pray, go into your room and shut the door and pray to your Father who is in secret. And your Father who sees in secret will reward you" (ESV). Interestingly, these Bible verses endorse a ritual practice that would not be evolutionary beneficial on CST or AT because the prayer is not public.

65 Jong (2012).

66 Barrett and Church (2013).

67 Jong adds that some theological explanations, like creationism and intelligent design, are on the same level of explanation as evolutionary explanations and hence can stand in conflict with them.

68 He writes, "There is, of course, no guarantee that such an argument could be successful; there is no guarantee that it makes sense to ask questions about ultimate causes or that a theological explanation will turn out to be the best one for such questions. The evaluation of such theistic arguments are certainly beyond the scope of this current project, but must be undertaken for a fuller analysis of the implications of any naturalistic explanation of any phenomenon for theistic or religious belief" (Jong 2012: 528).

69 To my knowledge, Plantinga does not state this explicitly. Clark and Barrett probably have Plantinga's examples of the sensus divinitatis being triggered by contemplating nature or when reading Scripture in mind.

70 Clark and Barrett (2010). It is not immediately clear what Clark and Barrett mean with ignorance and terror as grounding conditions.

Maybe they have ignorance of what agents are around and fear of them in mind.
71　Clark and Barrett (2010).
72　See, for example, Rom. 1:20 "For since the creation of the world God's invisible qualities—his eternal power and divine nature—have been clearly seen, being understood from what has been made, so that people are without excuse" (NIV).

Chapter 5

1. This chapter is an adapted version of my paper "Is Supernatural Belief Unreliably Formed?" (Van Eyghen 2019).
2. Authors use different terms to refer to the *cognitive mechanisms* laid bare by CSR. Some use the term "mechanism" or "belief-forming mechanism." Other use "faculty" or "belief-forming process." All terms are interchangeable. I will use the term "mechanism" or "CSR mechanism."
3. He writes, "This suggests a general schema for a number of naturalistic hypotheses about how the operation of our minds can be claimed to cause religious belief" (Nola 2013: 163).
4. They write, "None of the contemporary evolutionary explanations of religious belief hypothesizes that those beliefs are produced by a mechanism that tracks truth" (Wilkins and Griffiths 2013: 141).
5. Braddock (2016: 269, emphasis added).
6. Braddock (2016, emphasis added).
7. Nola (2013, emphasis added).
8. Wilkins and Griffiths (2013, emphasis added).
9. Goodnick (2016, emphasis added).
10. Clark (2010: 514, emphasis added).
11. This response goes by different names. Lari Launonen calls it "the internalist response" (Launonen 2017), and Jonathan Jong and Aku Visala call it an "indirect Milvian bridge" (2014).
12. Jong and Visala don't refer to the arguments I discuss below but target "debunking arguments" in general.
13. Jong and Visala (2014).

14 Jong and Visala (2014).
15 McBrayer calls them "genealogical arguments."
16 McBrayer (2018).
17 Jong and Visala note that unreliability arguments could affect adherents of Reformed Epistemology (see: Plantinga 2000; Clark 1990). Adherents argue that believers do not need additional evidence to be justified in their supernatural beliefs. Jong and Visala thus suggest that even reformed epistemologists do not meet the required standards.
18 For criticisms, see: Philipse (2012) and Mackie (1982).
19 See, for example, de Bruin (2013).
20 De Cruz and De Smedt (2015). De Cruz and De Smedt do not conclude that CSR undermines arguments from natural theology but do conclude that their close connection allows for reasonable disagreement.
21 For an overview of the discussion, see: Poston (no date).
22 Jong and Visala (2014).
23 For example, Wilkins and Griffiths (2013).
24 In all likelihood, both do not agree on the force of additional reasons for supernatural belief.
25 Goodnick (2016: 26).
26 Whether the mechanisms are adaptations in themselves or by-products does not matter here. By-products were also selected for by natural selection along with the adaptations they hinge upon.
27 One line of criticism against Goodnick's and all unreliability arguments is that it is difficult (if not impossible) to show which processes or mechanisms produce a given belief or set of beliefs. This problem is known as the "Generality Problem" (Conee and Feldman 1998). This criticism does not seem valid against these arguments because the arguments I discuss here assess the reliability of processes or mechanisms and not the epistemic status of a given belief or set of beliefs. Concluding to the unreliability of a process or mechanism only casts doubts on the beliefs that are produced by it. I will indeed argue when criticizing Braddock's argument that it is not clear that the beliefs he targets are produced solely by the mechanisms he criticizes.
28 Barrett and Church (2013).
29 Clark and Barrett (2010).
30 Plantinga (2011: Chapter 5).

31 Wilkins and Griffiths (2013: 134). Readers familiar with evolutionary debunking arguments against morality will recognize the similarities with third factor responses (see Klenk 2018).
32 Justin McBrayer criticizes W&G's suspicion of skepticism and argues that belief-forming processes that have no correlation with what is true are false are neutral with respect to unreliability. He claims that only evidence that a belief-forming process is correlated with what is false can lend support for unreliability (McBrayer 2018).
33 The use of the term is an allusion to the battle at the Milvian Bridge in AD 312. Here Constantine beat his opponent Maxentius after having received a vision of the Christian God. According to the legend, Constantine won the battle because Christianity (or Christian beliefs) is true. In a similar way, (approximately) true common-sense beliefs would have beaten other beliefs in natural selection because they are true.
34 Wilkins and Griffiths (2013: 135).
35 Wilkins and Griffiths (2013: 155).
36 Wilkins and Griffiths (2013: 138).
37 Eddington (1930) quoted by Wilkins and Griffiths (2013: 138).
38 Wilkins and Griffiths (2013: 138, emphasis added).
39 Wilkins and Griffiths (2013: 138).
40 Wilkins and Griffiths (2013: 140). Bearing in mind their own line of reasoning, their claim is best rephrased as follows: "No Milvian bridge is available for supernatural beliefs, because none of the leading accounts of the evolution of supernatural belief makes any reference to them being constrained by reality when explaining their effects on reproductive fitness."
41 Wilkins and Griffiths (2013: 141).
42 Alston (1991) uses the term "mystical perceptions."
43 Alston (1991: 250–54).
44 Rik Peels argues that science depends to a large extent on common sense. In this view scientific beliefs are partly formed by the same cognitive mechanisms that produce common-sense beliefs (Peels 2017). Since Wilkins and Griffiths deny this point and I lack the time and space to assess it, I will not discuss this point any further.
45 I leave out "completely arbitrary" because no belief-forming mechanism is completely arbitrary. All mechanisms are constrained in some way.

What matters for Wilkins and Griffiths's argument is whether they are constrained by reality or not.
46 Campbell and Sedikides (1999: 23).
47 For a number of reasons it cannot be claimed that the bias is solely responsible for the production of beliefs. Other factors like the social environment and the proximate reasons that give rise to the belief also must be taken into account. In any case, the self-serving bias is still a major contributor to belief in personal merit and external blame and other factors are probably less important. This suffices for our purposes here.
48 Campbell and Sedikides (1999).
49 Koole (2009).
50 Braddock 2016: 270). I changed the numbers in the quotations.
51 Both camps echo William James's discussion in "The Will to Believe." He argues that people should strive to gain truths and avoid falsehoods. He notes that some will focus on gaining truths while others will emphasize avoiding falsehoods. The stricter camp appears to be motivated by an urge to avoid falsehoods. A mechanism of which we do not known whether it is reliable might produce false beliefs. The more lenient camp appears to be motivated by an urge to gain truths since a mechanism of which the status is unclear might produce truths.
52 Braddock (2016: 272).
53 Braddock (2016: 272, emphasis added).
54 Braddock (2016).
55 A recent study claimed that over 50 percent of the world population were either Christian or Muslim (Hackett and Grim 2012). To this Jews, a subset of Hindus, a subset of Buddhists, and some adherents of folk religions can be added. Nowadays, more people are monotheistic than polytheistic.
56 Braddock (2016). Barrett writes, "*In a certain respect*, believing in numerous superhuman agents appears to be the most natural type of belief system" (Barrett 2012a: 141–42) quoted by Braddock (2016: 274, emphasis added).

   Bloom writes, "There is no evidence that a belief in a single God . . . is unlearned. As best we know, such a belief is not a universal, and it does not emerge without social contact. . . . but these properties apply better

to supernatural belief more generally, not to belief in God" (Bloom 2009: 127) quoted by Braddock (2016: 274).
57 Barrett (2004a: 77).
58 Braddock (2016: 271).
59 Gervais and Henrich (2010).
60 Leech and Visala (2011a: 311). Leech and Visala refer to a standard model. I argued in Chapter 2 that speaking of a standard model in CSR is misleading. This is not essential for their argument.
61 Braddock responds to Leech and Visala's claim by limiting the scope of his argument. He argues that people who don't have access to other pathways still face a problem. He writes, "The dialectical context of the paper's question is this: if such arguments are not available (because the believer is not aware of them, or because there are no such convincing arguments), does the believer possess a defeater for her non-inferential belief?" He answers this question affirmatively (Braddock 2016: 277). By limiting the scope of his argument in this way, Braddock seems to acknowledge that Leech and Visala's response can help supernatural beliefs evade the charge of unreliability.
62 For a discussion of these theories and their philosophical implications, see, for example, Okasha (2013).
63 Lanman and Buhrmester (2017).
64 Henrich (2009).
65 Braddock (2016: 272).
66 See, for example, Margolis (1995) and Priest and Berto (2013).
67 Distinguishing gods from supernatural beings that are not gods is difficult and religious traditions appear to have different criteria. In general, gods appear to enjoy a higher standing than other supernatural beings. They are often considered regarded as more powerful or more worthy of praise. For the purposes of this chapter, it suffices that there is a distinction between gods and other supernatural beings.
68 Barrett (2012b).
69 The term "misattribution" is drawn from Luke Galen who makes an argument that closely resembles this one (Galen 2017). Other similar arguments were raised by Robert Nola (2013, 2018) and Stephen Law (2018). Robert Nola argues that the cognitive mechanisms for religious belief are "off-track." Stephen Law argues that human cognitive systems are making *erroneous* claims when they conclude to supernatural beings.

70 Ehrsson, Holmes, and Passingham (2005).
71 See, for example, "In scanning for such agents, we encounter false positives: we think we see agents where none exist" (Guthrie 2002: 1).
72 They write, "We have reviewed evidence suggesting that people believe in God . . . because they need to find a moral agent to account for their suffering" (Gray and Wegner 2010: 13). They also write, "The research reviewed in this article suggests that God may be more accurately characterized as 'God of the Moral Gaps,' a supernatural mind introduced into our perception of the world because of the underlying dyadic structure of morality" (Gray and Wegner 2010: 13–14).
73 Bering (2002a).
74 Boyer (2002).
75 Barrett (2004b: 40–41).
76 While many contemporary Christians are reluctant to attribute natural disasters directly to God's activity, there are passages in the Bible where God clearly causes disasters. The most famous is the great flood in Genesis 6–9.
77 Boudry, Blancke, and Braeckman (2010).
78 This argument has recently been criticized by Peter Harrison and myself (Harrison 2018; Van Eyghen 2018b).
79 Some scholars made several attempts to test Guthrie's and related theories, but most of his results did not support the claim that religious belief is formed after misidentifying natural input. See Van Leeuwen and Van Elk (2018: section 3.2) for a summary of the studies.
80 Barrett and Church (2013: 16–17).

Chapter 6

1 Some beliefs based on testimony might be affected if the testifier based her supernatural beliefs on religious experiences.
2 Swinburne (2004: 293).
3 Swinburne (2004: 303).
4 Swinburne (2004).
5 Swinburne (2004).

6 Swinburne (2004). Swinburne calls this "the principle of testimony."
7 He notes that opponents could deny that the principle of credulity is a fundamental valid epistemological principle. Opponents could argue that the principle itself requires inductive justification and that such justification is not available for religious experiences. Swinburne responds that inductive justification is often not available in ordinary cases, like experiences of tables, as well. Opponents could also argue that the principle of credulity only holds for (entities with) "sensible" characteristics and not for entities with "unsensible" characteristics like *unlimited* beings. Here Swinburne responds that a clear line between "sensible" and "unsensible characteristics cannot be drawn" (Swinburne 2004).
8 Swinburne (2004).
9 Graham Oppy claims that there is plenty of independent reason to suppose religious experiences are caused by a malfunctioning brain (Oppy 2006). Richard Dawkins claims that the human brain is easily deluded and suggests that religious experiences are one of the results (Dawkins 2007). John Mackie argues that religious experiences closely resemble hysteria, delusions, depressions where there is no religious component (Mackie 1982).
10 An example is found in Branden Thornhill-Miller and Peter Millican's paper "The Common-Core/Diversity Dilemma: Revisions of Humean Thought, New Empirical Research, and the Limits of Rational Religious Belief." They argue that recent empirical discoveries show that a cross-culturally common core of religious experiences can be explained naturalistically. This would undermine many religious beliefs (Thornhill-Miller and Millican 2015). On closer inspection, however, they discuss naturalistic explanations of near-death experiences and attributions of events to supernatural agents (REF). These are not religious experiences as we defined them but rather events that triggered the formation of religious belief.
11 Fales (1996a).
12 See Lewis (1989).
13 Fales (1996b).
14 Barrett (2007).
15 Murray (2008: 395–96).
16 Cf. Goldman (1967).

17 Leech and Visala (2011b).
18 Jong (2014) and Jong, Kavanagh, and Visala (2015).
19 Fingelkurts and Fingelkurts (2009).
20 Booth, Koren, and Persinger (2005).
21 He writes, "My fundamental argument is that most false positives in agency detection can be seen as the result of top-down interference in a Bayesian system" (Andersen 2017: 1).
22 Andersen (2017).
23 Alan Baker distinguishes two kinds of parsimony. Quantitative parsimony states that theories should not postulate a greater number of entities than needed. Qualitative parsimony states that theories should not postulate more kinds of entities than required (Baker 2010). For my purposes, the distinction is less important because adding supernatural beings to CSR theories constitutes a breach of both quantitative and qualitative parsimony.
24 See, for example, Sober (1981).
25 Many religious beliefs likely depend on testimony as well. It is not unlikely that, for many, religious testimony depends on some religious experience as well. If the religious testimony depends on religious experiences and the argument succeeds, their beliefs are no longer justified. If the testimony depends on other reasons, their beliefs are untouched.
26 Murray (2009: 175). Murray's responds to arguments against religious beliefs and not religious experiences. The rationale of his response also applies to religious experiences.
27 A creator God and designer God are not quite the same, although they often appear to be the same in much philosophy of religion. A creator God brings about the existence of something, in this case of the universe. Usually, creation is considered to be *creatio ex nihilo,* where God brings about the universe out of nothing. A designer God brings structure to existing stuff, for example, by using existing matter or tweaking cosmological constants.
28 See, for example, Holder (2002).
29 For example, Paley (2006).
30 For intelligent design arguments, see Behe (1996) and Dembski (2002). For criticisms, see Koperski (2008), and Kitcher and Follette (1984).
31 See, for example, Shanks and Green (2011).
32 The discussion of criticisms against Persinger's theory is drawn from my paper "Spirit Beliefs Debunked" (Van Eyghen 2018c: 78).

33 Andersen (2017).
34 French et al. (2009).
35 Luhrmann (2012).
36 The authors also give examples of experiences of witchcraft. I omitted them because our focus is on religious experiences.
37 Van Leeuwen and Van Elk (2018).
38 Andersen (2017) and van Elk and Aleman (2017).
39 They also argue that predictive coding can explain prayer experiences (Van Elk and Aleman 2017). Since prayer experiences often involve experiences of a supernatural presence, I omitted them.
40 Van Elk and Aleman (2017: 16–17).

Chapter 7

1 My discussion of naturalism and supernaturalism below appeared in a slightly adapted version in my paper "The Retreat Argument" (Van Eyghen 2018b).
2 For an overview of some of the theses "naturalism" can designate, see Flanagan (2006), Papineau (2007), and (Rosenberg 1996).
3 Like Plantinga I take naturalism to be "the idea that there is no such person as God or anything like him; immaterial selves would be too much like God, who, after all, is himself an immaterial self" (Plantinga 2011: 319). I omitted immaterial souls because they play no role in supernatural beliefs or (as Plantinga notes) are covered by supernatural beliefs.
4 For example, Flew (1972).
5 Jinn can roughly be identified with spirits.
6 The Faery Wiccans, like many other neo-pagan groups, do not have a clear list of beliefs and are very liberal toward individual preferences in belief. Therefore, it is possible that some Faery Wiccans do accept supreme gods. The emphasis is, however, usually on other supernatural beings.
7 Plato (2006, emphasis added).
8 Cicero (1913: book I section 44).
9 Nonetheless, modern defenders still refer to the argument as the consensus gentium argument. To avoid adding confusion, I will also use the same name.

10 Below I will sometimes replace "being evidence for" with "making a claim more probable." Although a wide occurrence being evidence for a proposition is an epistemological claim rather than a claim about likelihoods of claims and is perhaps broader, my reformulation at least follows from the epistemological claim.
11 Goldman (1999: 357). Goldman discusses knowledge and not truth. However, most classical analyses of knowledge state that knowing a proposition requires that the proposition is true.
12 For example, Aviezer Tucker writes, "A consensus on beliefs in a concrete group over a certain period is a concrete event that can be explained by competing hypotheses. From an epistemic perspective, the most interesting such hypothesis is that knowledge is the best explanation of a consensus" (Tucker 2003: 501).
13 Meierding (1998).
14 Kelly (2011).
15 For overviews of criticisms of inference to the best explanation, see van Fraassen (1989: 143 section 3.1), Douven (2011), and Lipton (1993).
16 Hackett and Grim (2012)
17 Not believing that the Christian God exists does not make one a naturalist. Someone who does not believe in the Christian God might still believe in another supernatural being or supernatural force. Some people are agnostic and claim they do not know whether anything supernatural exists. Agnosticism about the supernatural is not the same as believing in the thesis that nothing supernatural exists.
18 Some authors, like Linda Zagzebski (2011), Who I discuss below argue that a wide prevalence of supernatural beliefs only provides defeasible evidence. A wide prevalence indeed does not provide insurmountable proof for supernaturalism. Defeasible evidence is, however, still evidence and this suffices for my purposes.
19 Zagzebski adds that some people might lack a desire for truth or succeeded in giving it up. Her example is Pyrrhonian skeptics. She does argue that even they recognized that skepticism is not natural since they went through extensive therapy to become skeptics and to maintain their skepticism (Zagzebski 2011: 23).
20 Zagzebski draws on work by William Alston and Richard Foley to make this point (Foley and Alston 1995; Alston 1993).

21 Zagzebski (2011: 23–31).
22 Zagzebski (2011).
23 I will not take a stance on whether testimony reduces to other sources of evidence. Epistemologists have long discussed whether justification (or warrant or knowledge) from testimony reduces to other sources like perception. For an introduction to this discussion, see Adler (2006). A similar question can be asked of the evidential value of testimony. My second claim suggests that the evidential value of testimony does reduce to the evidential value of the evidence and experiences of the testifiers. Answering the question whether this is the case or whether this is always the case lies beyond the scope of this chapter.
24 Kelly (2011).
25 She could still smell a tree's flowers or hear the wind rustling through a tree's leaves. Since she lacks a clear picture of a tree, she will arguably not be able to draw a link between these smells and sounds and trees.
26 For a discussion of possible mechanisms that produce beliefs of this sort, see Van Elk (2013) and Bader, Mencken, and Baker (2011).
27 Elsewhere, René van Woudenberg and myself argue that this claim does not always hold. We argue that the low occurrence of belief in God among academic philosophers does not support the conclusion that belief in God is probably false. This is (among other reasons) because the higher occurrence of atheistic beliefs among these philosophers does not seem to reflect their evidence and experiences (Van Woudenberg and Van Eyghen 2017).
28 See, for example, Davidson (2013).
29 Swinburne (1993: 274–77).
30 Mill (1998: 155–56).
31 Locke also denies that belief in God is widely prevalent. He notes the existence of atheism among ancient philosophers. He also claims that many people in Brazil, China and the Caribbean island have been found who do not believe in God (Locke 1979: book I, chapter IV, section 8).
32 Locke (1979: book I, chapter IV, section 8).
33 See, for example, Kelly (2011: 2).
34 Locke (1979: book I, chapter IV, section 14).
35 Hume (1976: section XII–XII)
36 Kelly (2011: 20).

37 I draw the term from O' Dwyer (2015).
38 Kelly (2011).
39 See Chapter 5.
40 See Basinger (2015) for an overview.
41 A similar, less elaborated objection is discussed by Thomas Kelly (2011).
42 Zagzebski (2011: 38).
43 Zagzebski (2011: 41).
44 Kelly (2011: 8).
45 Kelly writes about epistemic significance rather than evidential significance. I phrase my first claim in terms of widely prevalent beliefs being evidence for a claim rather than providing justification (see above). Therefore, I reformulated Kelly's claim too.
46 "Wanneer het type verklaringen voor het ontstaan van religie zoals CSR die biedt in beginsel correct zouden zijn . . . [zou het] betekenen dat er een *alternatieve* verklaring voorhanden is voor het ontstaan van religie, zodat het zogeheten *argumentum e consensu gentium* ('je kunt toch wel zien dat er een god moet zijn, want alle volken zijn religieus') niet meer opgaat" (Van den Brink 2015: 125).
47 This group of scholars is known as defenders of intelligent design (e.g., Behe 1996; Dembski 2002). They claim that the complexity we see in nature requires design and could not have arisen by naturalistic means. Their views are highly controversial.
48 This claim is known as methodological naturalism.
49 The BGT (see Section 2.2.2) could also explain the *wide* occurrence of supernatural belief but in a somewhat different way. On this theory, belief in punishing gods became dominant after the Neolithic Revolution. On this theory, this substantial supernatural belief spread because of the advantage it yielded in cultural evolution.
50 Lim's use of the term is inspired by Robert Nola's term "folk explanation" (Nola 2013: 162).
51 Lim (2016).
52 Theists could also add that God explains why there is a world with humans and evolution at all. This response resembles the objection I discussed in Section 6.3.1. I believe the response runs into the same problems as the response I discussed there.
53 David Leech and Aku Visala argue that theists can claim that God set up human cognitive systems in such a way that they produce true beliefs. The

causal connection would be there but would be indirect. Leech and Visala add that an indirect stance might make God a deceiver because his causal influence seems direct to believers (Leech and Visala 2011b). Kelly Clark and Justin Barrett argue that CSR theories might show that God is not the *proximate* cause of supernatural beliefs, but do not show that God is not the *ultimate* cause (Clark and Barrett 2010).

54 Alan Baker distinguishes two kinds of parsimony. Quantitative parsimony states that theories should not postulate a greater number of entities than needed. Qualitative parsimony states that theories should not postulate more kinds of entities than required (Baker 2010).
55 See, for example, Sober (2001).
56 For example, adaptationist theories could explain why supernatural beliefs are in an individual's model of the world in the predictive coding framework. Because of the adaptive use of having supernatural beliefs, people could then be more prone to have religious experiences. The connection between adaptationist theories and predictive coding has, however, not been developped in detail.
57 De Cruz and De Smedt (2015).

References

Adler, Jonathan. 2006. "Epistemological Problems of Testimony." http://plato.stanford.edu/archives/spr2015/entries/testimony-episprob/.

Alston, William P. 1991. *Perceiving God: The Epistemology of Religious Experience* (Ithaca, NY: Cornell University Press).

Alston, William P. 1993. *The Reliability of Sense Perception* (Ithaca, NY: Cornell University Press).

Anderson, Benedict. 2004. *Imagined Communities: Reflections on the Origin and Spread of Nationalism* (London: Verso).

Andersen, Marc. 2017. "Predictive Coding in Agency Detection," *Religion, Brain & Behavior*, 9 (1): 65–84.

Asma, Lieke. 2017. "There Is No Free Won't: The Role Definitions Play," *Journal of Consciousness Studies*, 24: 8–23.

Asprem, Egil. 2017. "Explaining the Esoteric Imagination," *Aries*, 17: 17–50.

Atran, Scott. 2002. *In Gods We Trust: The Evolutionary Landscape of Religion* (Oxford: Oxford University Press).

Atran, Scott, and Joseph Henrich. 2010. "The Evolution of Religion: How Cognitive By-Products, Adaptive Learning Heuristics, Ritual Displays, and Group Competition Generate Deep Commitments to Prosocial Religions," *Biological Theory*, 5: 18–30.

Azari, Nina P., Janpeter Nickel, Gilbert Wunderlich, Michael Niedeggen, Harald Hefter, Lutz Tellman, Hans Herzog, Petra Stoerig, Dieter Birnbacher, and Rudiger J. Seitz. 2001. "Neural Correlates of Religious Experience," *European Journal of Neuroscience*, 13: 1649–52.

Bader, Christopher, F. Carson Mencken, and Joseph O. Baker. 2011. *Paranormal America: Ghost Encounters, UFO Sightings, Bigfoot Hunts, and Other Curiosities in Religion and Culture* (New York and London: New York University Press).

Baker, Alan. 2010. "Simplicity." Accessed December 8, 2016. https://plato.stanford.edu/archives/fall2013/entries/simplicity/.

Baldwin, Erik, and Michael Thune. 2008. "The Epistemological Limits of Experience-Based Exclusive Religious Belief," *Religious Studies*, 44: 445–55.

Barrett, Justin L. 1998. "Cognitive Constraints on Hindu Concepts of the Divine," *Journal for the Scientific Study of Religion*, 37: 608–19.

Barrett, Justin L. 1999. "Theological Correctness: Cognitive Constraint and the Study of Religion," *Method & Theory in the Study of Religion*, 11: 325–39.

Barrett, Justin L. 2004a. "The Naturalness of Religious Concepts," *New Approaches to the Study of Religion*, 2: 401–18.

Barrett, Justin L. 2004b. *Why Would Anyone Believe in God?* (Walnut Creek: Altamira Press).

Barrett, Justin L. 2007. "Is the Spell Really Broken? Biopsychological Explanations of Religion and Theistic Belief," *Theology and Science*, 5: 57–72.

Barrett, Justin L. 2012a. *Born Believers: The Science of Children's Religious Belief* (New York: Free Press).

Barrett, Justin L. 2012b. "Towards a Cognitive Science of Christianity," in J. B. Stump and Alan G. Padgett (eds.), *The Blackwell Companion to Science and Christianity* (Oxford: Blackwell Publishing).

Barrett, Justin L., and Ian M. Church. 2013. "Should CSR Give Atheists Epistemic Assurance? On Beer-goggles, BFFs, and Skepticism Regarding Religious Belief," *The Monist*, 96: 311–24.

Barth, Karl. 1957. *Die kirchliche Dogmatik* (Zürich: Theologischer Verlag Zürich).

Basinger, David. 2015. "Religious Diversity (Pluralism)." Accessed December 1, 2016. http://plato.stanford.edu/archives/win2016/entries/religious-pluralism/.

Baumard, Nicolas, and Pascal Boyer. 2013. "Explaining Moral Religions," *Trends in Cognitive Sciences*, 17: 272–80.

Beauregard, Mario, and Vincent Paquette. 2006. "Neural Correlates of a Mystical Experience in Carmelite Nuns," *Neuroscience Letters*, 405: 186–90.

Behe, Michael J. 1996. *Darwin's Black Box: The Biochemical Challenge to Evolution* (New York: Simon and Schuster).

Beheim, Bret, Quentin Atkinson, Joseph Bulbulia, Will M. Gervais, Russell Gray, Joseph Henrich, Martin Lang, M Willis Monroe, Michael Muthukrishna, and Ara Norenzayan. forthcoming. "Corrected Analyses Show That Moralizing Gods Precede Complex Societies but Serious Data Concerns Remain," *PsyArXiv*.

Bek, Judith, and Suzanne Lock. 2011. "Afterlife Beliefs: Category Specificity and Sensitivity to Biological Priming," *Religion, Brain & Behavior*, 1: 5–17.

Bering, Jesse. 2002a. "The Existential Theory of Mind," *Review of General Psychology*, 6: 3–24.

Bering, Jesse. 2002b. "Intuitive Conceptions of Dead Agents' Minds: The Natural Foundations of Afterlife Beliefs as Phenomenological Boundary," *Journal of Cognition and Culture*, 2: 263–308.

Bering, Jesse M. 2002c. "The Existential Theory of Mind," *Review of General Psychology*, 6: 3–24.

Bering, Jesse. 2012. *The Belief Instinct: The Psychology of Souls, Destiny, and the Meaning of Life* (London: Nicholas Brealey Publishing).

Bering, Jesse, and David F. Bjorklund. 2004. "The Natural Emergence of Reasoning About the Afterlife as a Developmental Regularity," *Developmental Psychology*, 40: 217–34.

Bering, Jesse, and Dominic Johnson. 2005. "'O Lord . . . You Perceive My Thoughts from Afar': Recursiveness and the Evolution of Supernatural Agency," *Journal of Cognition and Culture*, 5: 118–43.

Bering, Jesse, J. Piazza, and G. Ingram. 2011. "'Princess Alice Is Watching You': Children's Belief in an Invisible Person Inhibits Cheating," *Journal of Experimental Child Psychology*, 109: 311–20.

Bloom, Paul. 2004. *Descartes' Baby: How the Science of Child Development Explains What Makes Us Human* (New York: Basic Books).

Bloom, Paul. 2005. "Is God an Accident?," *The Atlantic Monthly*, December.

Bloom, Paul. 2007. "Religion Is Natural," *Developmental Science*, 10: 147–51.

Bloom, Paul. 2009. "Religious Belief as an Evolutionary Accident," in Michael Murray and Jeffrey Schloss (eds.), *The Believing Primate* (New York: Oxford University Press).

Bogen, Jim. 2013. "Theory and Observation in Science." http://plato.stanford.edu/archives/sum2014/entries/science-theory-observation/.

Booth, J. N., S. Koren, and M. A. Persinger. 2005. "Increased Feelings of the Sensed Presence and Increased Geomagnetic Activity at the Time of the Experience During Exposures to Transcerebral Weak Complex Magnetic Fields," *International Journal for Neuroscience*, 115: 1053–79.

Booth, J. N., and M. A. Persinger. 2009. "Discrete Shifts Within the Theta Band Between the Frontal and Parietal Regions of the Right Hemisphere and the Experiences of a Sensed Presence," *Journal of Neuropsychiatry*, 21: 279–83.

Boudry, Maarten. 2018. "Dying for Your Group or for Your Faith? On the Power of Belief," *Behavioral and Brain Sciences*, 41: e195.

Boudry, Maarten, Stefaan Blancke, and Johan Braeckman. 2010. "How Not to Attack Intelligent Design Creationism: Philosophical Misconceptions About Methodological Naturalism," *Foundations of Science*, 15: 227–44.

Bourget, David, and David J. Chalmers. 2013. "What Do Philosophers Believe?," *Philosophical Studies*, 170 (3): 465–500.

Boyer, Pascal. 2002. *Religion Explained: The Human Instincts That Fashion Gods, Spirits and Ancestors* (London: Vintage).

Boyer, Pascal. 2003. "Religious Thought and Behaviour as By-Products of Brain Function," *Trends in Cognitive Sciences*, 7: 119–25.

Boyer, Pascal. 2004. "Why Is Religion Natural?," *Skeptical Enquirer*, 28: 1–7.

Boyer, Pascal, and Pierre Liénard. 2006. "Why Ritualized Behavior? Precaution Systems and Action Parsing in Developmental, Pathological and Cultural Rituals," *Behavioral and Brain Sciences*, 29: 595–613.

Braddock, Matthew. 2016. "Debunking Arguments and the Cognitive Science of Religion," *Theology and Science*, 14: 268–87.

Bulbulia, Joseph, and Richard Sosis. 2011. "Signalling Theory and the Evolution of Religious Cooperation," *Religion*, 41: 363–88.

Bulbulia, Joseph, John H. Shaver, Lara M. Greaves, Richard Sosis, and Chris G. Sibley. 2015. "Religion and Parental Cooperation: An Empirical Test of Slone & Van Slyke's Sexual Signaling Model," in D. Jason Slone and James A. Van Slyke (eds.), *The Attraction of Religion: A New Evolutionary Psychology of Religion* (London: Bloomsbury Academic).

Campbell, W. Keith, and Constantine Sedikides. 1999. "Self-Threat Magnifies the Self-Serving-Bias: A Meta-analytic Integration," *Review of General Psychology*, 3: 23–43.

Carruthers, Peter. 1996. "Simulation and Self-Knowledge: A Defence of Theory-Theory," in Peter Carruthers and Peter K. Smith (eds.), *Theories of Theories of Mind* (Cambridge: Cambridge University Press).

Casler, Krista, and Deborah Kelemen. 2008. "Developmental Continuity in Teleo-Functional Explanation: Reasoning About Nature Among Romanian Romani Adults," *Journal of Cognition and Development*, 9: 340–62.

Cicero, Marcus Tullius. 1913. *De Natura Deorum; Academica* (Cambridge, MA and London: Harvard University Press and W. Heinemann:).

Clark, Andy. 2013. "Whatever Next? Predictive Brains, Situated Agents, and the Future of Cognitive science," *Behavioral and Brain Sciences*, 36: 181–204.

Clark, Kelly James. 1990. *Return to Reason: A Critique of Enlightenment Evidentialism and a Defense of Reason and Belief in God* (Grand Rapids, Michigan: Eerdmans).

Clark, Kelly James. 2010. "Explaining God Away?" in *Science and Religion in Dialogue*, edited by Melville Y. Stewart, 514–26 (Oxford: Wiley-Blackwell).

Clark, Kelly James, and Dani Rabinowitz. 2011. "Knowledge and the Objection to Religious Belief from Cognitive Science," *European Journal for Philosophy of Religion*, 3: 67–81.

Clark, Kelly James, and Justin L. Barrett. 2010. "Reformed Epistemology and the Cognitive Science of Religion," *Faith and Philosophy*, 27: 174–89.

Cohen, Emma, Roger Mundry, and Sebastian Kirschner. 2014. "Religion, Synchrony, and Cooperation," *Religion, Brain & Behavior*, 4: 20–30.

Conee, E., and R. Feldman. 1998. "The Generality Problem for Reliabilism," *Philosophical Studies*, 89: 1–29.

Craig, William Lane. 2001. *Time and Eternity: Exploring God's Relationship to Time* (Wheaton, IL: Crossway).

Cuneo, Terence. 2014. "Ritual Knowledge," *Faith and Philosophy*, 31: 365–85.

Cuneo, Terence, and Russ Shafer-Landau. 2014. "The Moral Fixed Points: New Directions for Moral Nonnaturalism," *Philosophical Studies*, 171: 399–443.

Davidson, Matthew. 2013. "God and Other Necessary Beings." Accessed January 13, 2017. https://plato.stanford.edu/archives/spr2015/entries/god-necessary-being/.

Davis, Stephen T. 1993. "Passing the Baton," in Kelly James Clark (ed.), *Philosophers Who Believe: The Spiritual Journeys of 11 Leading Thinkers* (Downers Grove, IL: InterVarsity Press).

Dawkins, Richard. 2007. *The God Delusion* (London: Blackswan).

de Bruin, Boudewijn. 2013. "The Epistemology of Religious Testimony," *Philo*, 16: 95–111.

De Cruz, Helen. 2018. "Etiological Challenges to Religious Practices," *American Philosophical Quarterly*, 55 (4): 329–40.

De Cruz, Helen, and Johan De Smedt. 2015. *A Natural History of Natural Theology. The Cognitive Science of Theology and Philosophy of Religion* (Cambridge and London: MIT Press).

De Cruz, Helen, Maarten Boudry, Johan De Smedt, and Stefaan Blancke. 2011. "Evolutionary Approaches to Epistemic Justification," *Dialectica*, 65: 517–35.

DeBono, A., A. F. Shariff, and M. Muraven. 2012. "Forgive Us Our Trespasses: Priming a Forgiving (but Not a Punishing) God Increases Theft," *Psychology of Religion and Spirituality*, 9 (Suppl 1): S1–S10.

Dembski, William A. 2002. *No Free Lunch: Why Specified Complexity Cannot Be Purchased Without Intelligence* (Lanham: Rowman & Littlefield).

Dennett, Daniel Clement. 2006. *Breaking the Spell: Religion as a Natural Phenomenon* (New York: Penguin).

de Ridder Jeroen. 2011. "Religious Exclusivism Unlimited," *Religious Studies*, 47: 449–63.

de Ridder, Jeroen, and Mathanja Berger. 2013. "Shipwrecked or Holding Water? In Defense of Alvin Plantinga's Warranted Christian Believer," *Philo*, 16: 42–61.

de Ridder, Jeroen, and René van Woudenberg. 2014. "Referring to, Believing in, and Worshipping the Same God: A Reformed View," *Faith and Philosophy*, 31: 46–67.

Douven, Igor. 2011. "Abduction." Accessed January 20, 2017. https://plato.stanford.edu/entries/abduction/.

Dubuisson, Daniel. 2007. "Exporting the Local: Recent Perspectives on 'Religion' as a Cultural Category," *Religion Compass*, 1: 787–800.

Dundas, Paul. 2004. "Beyond Anekāntavāda: A Jain Approach to Religious Tolerance," in Tara Sethia (ed.), *Ahiṃsā, Anekānta, and Jaininsm* (Delhi: Motilal Banarsidass).

Eddington, A. S. 1930. *The Nature of the Physical World* (Cambridge: Cambridge University Press).

Edelman, Benjamin. 2009. "Red Light States: Who Buys Online Adult Entertainment?," *The Journal of Economic Perspectives*, 23: 209–20.

Ehrsson, H. Henrik, Nicholas, P. Holmes, and Richard E. Passingham. 2005. "Touching a Rubber Hand: Feeling of Body Ownership Is Associated with Activity in Multisensory Brain Areas," *Journal of Neuroscience*, 25: 10564–73.

Evans, E. Margaret. 2000. "The Emergence of Beliefs About the Origins of Species in School-Age Children," *Merrill-Palmer Quarterly (1982-)*, 46: 221–54.

Fales, Evan. 1996a. "Scientific Explanations of Mystical Experiences Part I: The Case of St Teresa," *Religious Studies*, 32: 143–63.

Fales, Evan. 1996b. "Scientific Explanations of Mystical Experiences: II: The Challenge of Theism," *Religious Studies*, 32: 297–313.

Ferrari, Fabrizio M. 2014. *Religion, Devotion and Medicine in North India: The Healing Power of Sitala* (London: Bloomsbury).

Fingelkurts, A. A., and A. A. Fingelkurts. 2009. "Is Our Brain Hardwired to Produce God, or Is Our Brain Hardwired to Perceive God? A Systematic Review on the Role of the Brain in Mediating Religious Experience," *Cognitive Processing*, 10 (4): 293–326.

FitzPatrick, William J. 2015. "Debunking Evolutionary Debunking of Ethical Realism," *Philosophical Studies*, 172: 883–904.

Flanagan, Owen. 2006. "Varieties of Naturalism," in P. Clayton, Z. Simpson, (eds.), *The Oxford Handbook of Religion and Science* (New York: Oxford University Press on Demand).

Flew, Antony. 1972. "The Presumption of Atheism," *Canadian Journal of Philosophy*, 2: 29–46.

Foley, Richard, and William P. Alston. 1995. "The Reliability of Sense Perception," *Philosophical Review*, 104: 133.

French, C. C., U. Haque, R. Bunton-Stasyshyn, and R. Davis. 2009. "The 'Haunt' Project: An Attempt to Build a 'Haunted' Room by Manipulating Complex Electromagnetic Fields and Infrasound," *cortex*, 45 (5): 619–29.

Freud, Sigmund Schlomo. 1961. *The Future of an Illusion; Civilization and Its Discontents and Other Works* (London: Hogarth Press).

Friston, Karl. 2010. "The Free-Energy Principle: A Unified Brain Theory?," *Nature Reviews Neuroscience*, 11: 127.

Galen, Luke. 2017. "Overlapping Mental Magisteria: Implications of Experimental Psychology for a Theory of Religious Belief as Misattribution," *Method & Theory in the Study of Religion*, 29: 221–67.

Ganssle, Gregory E. 2001. *God & Time: Four Views* (Downers Grove, IL: InterVarsity Press cop.).

Gervais, Will, and Joseph Henrich. 2010. "The Zeus Problem: Why Representational Content Biases Cannot Explain Faith in Gods," *Journal of Cognition and Culture*, 10: 383–89.

Gervais, Will M. 2013. "In Godlessness We Distrust: Using Social Psychology to Solve the Puzzle of Anti-Atheist Prejudice," *Social and Personality Psychology Compass*, 7: 366–77.

Gervais, Will M., and A. Norenzayan. 2012a. "Like a Camera in the Sky? Thinking About God Increases Public Self-Awareness and Socially Desirable Responding," *Journal of Experimental Social Psychology*, 48: 298–302.

Gervais, Will, and A. Norenzayan. 2012b. "Analytic Thinking Promotes Religious Disbelief," *Science*, 336, 493–96.

Gilbert, Paul. 1998. "What Is Shame? Some Core Issues and Controversies," in P. Gilbert and B. Andrews (eds.), *Shame: Interpersonal Behavior, Psychopathology, and Culture. Series in Affective Science* (New York: Oxford University Press).

Goldman, Alvin I. 1967. "A Causal Theory of Knowing," *The Journal of Philosophy*, 64: 357–72.

Goldman, Alvin I. 1999. *Knowledge in a Social World*. (Oxford and New York: Clarendon Press and Oxford University Press).

Goodnick, Liz. 2016. "A De Jure Criticism of Theism," *Open Theology*, 2: 23–33.

Gopnik, Alison, Andrew N. Meltzoff, and Patricia K. Kuhl. 1999. *The Scientist in the Crib: Minds, Brains, and How Children Learn* (New York: William Morrow & Co).

Granqvist, P., M. Fredrikson, P. Unge, A. Hagenfeldt, S. Valind, D. Larhammar, and M. Larsson. 2005. "Sensed Presence and Mystical Experiences Are Predicted by Suggestibility, Not by the Application of Transcranial Weak Complex Magnetic Fields," *Neuroscience Letters*, 379: 1–6.

Gray, Heather M., Kurt Gray, and Daniel M. Wegner. 2007. "Dimensions of Mind Perception," *Science*, 315: 619–19.

Gray, Kurt, and Daniel M. Wegner. 2010. "Blaming God for Our Pain: Human Suffering and the Divine Mind," *Personality and Social Psychology Review*, 14: 7–16.

Gray, Kurt, and Daniel M. Wegner. 2011. "Morality Takes Two: Dyadic Morality and Mind Perception," *The Social Psychology of Morality: Exploring the Causes of Good and Evil*: 109–27.

Greene, Joshua D. 2014. "Beyond Point-and-Shoot Morality: Why Cognitive (Neuro)Science Matters for Ethics," *Ethics*, 124: 695–726.

Guthrie, Stewart. 2002. "Animal Animism: Evolutionary Roots of Religious Cognition," in Ilkka Pyysiainen and Veikko Anttonen (eds.), *Current Approaches in the Cognitive Science of Religion*, 38–67 (London: Continuum).

Guthrie, Stewart Elliott. 2007. "Anthropology and Anthropomorphism in Religion," in Harvey Whitehouse and James Laidlaw (eds.), *Religion, Anthropology, and Cognitive Science* (Durham, NC: Carolina Academic Press).

Hackett, Conrad, and Brian J. Grim. 2012. "The Global Religious Landscape: A Report on the Size and Distribution of the World's Major Religious Groups as of 2010." The Pew Research Center. Accessed November 28, 2016.

Hall, Deborah L., David C. Matz, and Wendy Wood. 2010. "Why Don't We Practice What We Preach? A Meta-Analytic Review of Religious Racism," *Personality and Social Psychology Review*, 14: 126–39.

Harrison, Peter. 2018. "Naturalism and the Success of Science," *Religious Studies*: 1–18.

Hawkins, Jeff, and Sandra Blakeslee. 2004. *On intelligence* (New York: St. Martins Griffin).

Hayes, Glen Alexander, and Sthaneshwar Timalsina. 2017. "Introduction to 'Cognitive Science and the Study of Yoga and Tantra,'" *Religions*, 8: 181.

Henrich, Joseph. 2009. "The Evolution of Costly Displays, Cooperation and Religion: Credibility Enhancing Displays and Their Implications for Cultural Evolution," *Evolution and Human Behavior*, 30: 244–60.

Hick, John. 1974. *Evil and the God of Love* (London: Fontana).

Hodge, K. Mitch. 2016. "The Death We Fear Is Not Our Own: The Folk Psychology of Souls Revisited and Reframed," in Helen De Cruz and Ryan Nichols (eds.), *Advances in Religion, Cognitive Science, and Experimental Philosophy* (London: Bloomsbury Academic).

Hodge, K.Mitch, Paolo Sousa, and Claire White. unpublished. "Proposed Cognitive Mechanisms and Representational Structures of Afterlife Beliefs: A Review."

Holder, Rodney D. 2002. "Fine-Tuning, Multiple Universes and Theism," *Noûs*, 36: 295–312.

Howard-Snyder, Daniel. 1996. *The Evidential Argument from Evil* (Bloomington: Indiana University Press).

Hume, David. 1976. *The Natural History of Religion* (Oxford: Clarendon).

Ianneconne, Laurence R. 1992. "Sacrifice and Stigma: Reducing Free-Riding in Cults, Communes and Other Collectives," *Journal of Political Economy*, 100: 271–91.

Irons, William. 2001. "Religion as a Hard-to-Fake-Sign of Commitment," in R. Nesse (ed.), Evolution and the Capacity for Commitment (New York: Russell Sage Foundation).

James, W. 1902. *The Varieties of Religious Experience* (Cambridge, MA: Harvard University Press).

James, W. 1956. *The will to believe*: And other essays in popular philosophy, and Human immortality. Vol. 291. (Courier Corporation).

Johnson, Dominic, and Jesse Bering. 2009. "Hand of God, Mind of Man," in Jeffrey Schloss and Michael J. Murray (eds.), *The Believing Primate: Scientific, Philosophical, and Theological Reflections on the Origin of Religion* (Oxford: Oxford University Press).

Jones, James W. 2016. *Can Science Explain Religion? The Cognitive Science Debate* (Oxford: Oxford University Press).

Jong, Jonathan. 2012. "Explaining Religion (Away?) Theism and the Cognitive Science of Religion," *Sophia*, 52: 521–33.

Jong, Jonathan. 2014. "How Not to Criticize the (Evolutionary) Cognitive Science of Religion." Accessed July 9, 2015. http://marginalia.lareviewofbooks.org/criticize-evolutionary-cognitive-science-religion/.

Jong, Jonathan, and Aku Visala. 2014. "Evolutionary Debunking Arguments Against Theism, Reconsidered," *International Journal for Philosophy of Religion*, 76: 243–58.

Jong, Jonathan, Christopher Kavanagh, and Aku Visala. 2015. "Born Idolaters: The Limits of the Philosophical Implications of the Cognitive Science of Religion," *Neue Zeitschrift für Systematische Theologie und Religionsphilosophie*, 57: 244–66.

Joyce, Richard. 2007. *The Evolution of Morality* (Cambridge, MA: MIT Press).

Kahane, Guy. 2011. "Evolutionary Debunking Arguments," *Noûs*, 45: 103–25.

Kahneman, Daniel. 2012. *Thinking, Fast and Slow* (Penguin: London).

Kelemen, Deborah. 1999. "Why Are Rocks Pointy? Children's Preference for Teleological Explanations of the Natural World," *Developmental Psychology*, 35: 1440.

Kelemen, Deborah. 2003. "British and American Children's Preferences for Teleo-Functional Explanations of the Natural World," *Cognition*, 88: 201–21.

Kelemen, Deborah. 2004. "Are Children 'Intuitive Theists'?: Reasoning About Purpose and Design in Nature," *Psychological Science*, 15: 295–301.

Kelemen, Deborah, and Evelyn Rosset. 2009. "The Human Function Compunction: Teleological Explanation in Adults," *Cognition*, 111: 138–43.

Kelly, Thomas. 2011. "Consensus Gentium: Reflections on the 'Common Consent' Argument for the Existence of God," in Kelly James Clark and Raymond J. Van Arragon (eds.), *Evidence and Religious Belief* (Oxford: Oxford University Press).

Kieckhefer, Richard. 1978. "Meister Eckhart's Conception of Union with God," *The Harvard Theological Review*, 71: 203–25.

Kitcher, Philip, and Marcel C. La Follette. 1984. "Abusing Science: The Case against Creationism." *Journal of the History of Biology* 17 (1): 147–48.

Klenk, Michael. 2018. "Third Factor Explanations and Disagreement in Metaethics," *Synthese*: 1–20.

Koole, Sander L. 2009. "The Psychology of Emotion Regulation: An Integrative Review," *Cognition and Emotion*, 23: 4–41.

Koperski, J. 2008. "Two Bad Ways to Attack Intelligent Design and Two Good Ones," *Zygon®*, 43 (2): 433–49.

Kwan, Kai. 2009. "The Argument from Religious Experience," in William Lane Craig and James Porter Moreland (eds.), *The Blackwell Companion to Natural Theology* (Malden: Wiley-Blackwell).

Kyriacou, Christos. 2017. "Expressivism, Question Substitution and Evolutionary Debunking," *Philosophical Psychology*, 30: 1019–42.

Ladyman, James. 2011. "The Scientific Stance: The Empirical and Materialist Stances Reconciled," *Synthese*, 178: 87–98.

Lane, J., Z. Liqi, E. M. Evans, and H. M. Wellman. 2016. "Developing Concepts of Mind, Body and Afterlife: Exploring the Roles of Narrative Context and Culture," *Journal of Cognition and Culture*: 16 (1) 50–82.

Lanman, Jonathan A, and Michael D Buhrmester. 2017. "Religious Actions Speak Louder than Words: Exposure to Credibility-Enhancing Displays Predicts Theism," *Religion, Brain & Behavior*, 7: 3–16.

Launonen, Lari Tapani. 2017. "Cognitive Science of Religion and the Debunking Debate," in *The Origin of Religion: Perspectives from Philosophy, Theology, and Religious Studies* (Helsinki: Luther-Agricola-Society).

Law, Stephen. 2018. "The X-Claim Argument Against Religious Belief," *Religious Studies*, 54: 15–35.

Lawson, E. Thomas, and Robert N. McCauley. 1990. *Rethinking Religion: Connecting Cognition and Culture* (Cambridge: Cambridge University Press).

Leech, David, and Aku Visala. 2011a. "The Cognitive Science of Religion: A Modified Theist Response," *Religious Studies*, 47: 301–16.

Leech, David, and Aku Visala. 2011b. "The Cognitive Science of Religion: Implications for Theism?," *Zygon*, 46: 47–65.

Lewis, I. M. 1989. *Ecstatic Religion: A Study of Shamanism and Spirit Possession* (London: Routledge).

Libet, Benjamin. 1985. "Unconscious Cerebral Initiative and the Role of Conscious Will in Voluntary Action," *Behavioral and Brain Sciences*, 8: 529–66.

Lim, Daniel. 2016. "Cognitive Science of Religion and Folk Theistic Belief," *Zygon*, 51: 949–65.

Lindeman, Marjaana, Annika M. Svedholm-Häkkinen, and Jari Lipsanen. 2015. "Ontological Confusions but Not Mentalizing Abilities Predict Religious Belief, Paranormal Belief, and Belief in Supernatural Purpose," *Cognition*, 134: 63–76.

Lipton, Peter. 1993. "Is the Best Good Enough?," *Proceedings of the Aristotelian Society*, 93: 89–104.

Locke, John. 1979. *An Essay Concerning Human Understanding* (Oxford: Clarendon Press).

Luhrmann, Tanya M. 2012. *When God Talks Back: Understanding the American Evangelical Relationship with God* (New York: Vintage).

Mackie, John Leslie. 1982. *The Miracle of Theism: Arguments For and Against the Existence of God* (New York: Oxford University Press).

Malhotra, Deepak K. 2008. "(When) Are Religious People Nicer? Religious Salience and the 'Sunday Effect' on Pro-social Behavior," *Religious Salience and the "Sunday Effect" on Pro-social Behavior (November 6, 2008)*. Harvard Business School NOM Working Paper.

Margolis, Joseph Zalman. 1995. *Historied Thought, Constructed World: Conceptual Primer for the Turn of the Millennium* (Berkeley: University of California Press).

Martin, Luther H., and Donald Wiebe. 2014. "Pro-and Assortative-Sociality in the Formation and Maintenance of Religious Groups," *Journal for the Cognitive Science of Religion*, 2: 42–48.

Martinez, Matthew, and Pierre Lienard. 2015. "The Dividends of Discounting Pain: Self-Inflicted Pain as a Reputational Commodity," in D. Jason Slone and James A. Van Slyke (eds.), *The Attraction of Religion: A New Evolutionary Psychology of Religion* (London: Bloomsbury Academic).

Mazar, Nina, On Amir, and Dan Ariely. 2008. "The Dishonesty of Honest People: A Theory of Self-Concept Maintenance," *Journal of Marketing Research*, 45: 633–44.

McBrayer, Justin P. 2018. "The Epistemology of Genealogies," in Hans van Eyghen, Rik Peels and Gijsbert van den Brink (eds.), *New Developments in the Cognitive Science of Religion* (Dordrecht: Springer).

McCauley, Robert N. 2011. *Why Religion Is Natural and Science Is Not* (Oxford: Oxford University Press).

McCauley, Robert N. 2015. "Maturationally Natural Cognition, Radically Counter-Intuitive Science, and the Theory-Ladenness of Perception," *Journal for General Philosophy of Science*, 46: 183–99.

McCullough, Michael E., and Brian L. B. Willoughby. 2009. "Religion, Self-Regulation, and Self-Control: Associations, Explanations, and Implications," *Psychological Bulletin*, 135: 69–93.

Mckay, R., and H. Whitehouse. 2014. "Religion and Morality," *Psychological Bulletin*, 141: 447–73

McLaughlin, Brian, and Karen Bennett. 2005. "Supervenience," *The Stanford Encyclopedia of Philosophy* (Spring 2014 Edition).

Meierding, Loren. 1998. "The Consensus Gentium Argument," *Faith and Philosophy*, 15: 271–97.

Mill, John Stuart. 1998. "Theism," in *Three Essays on Religion: Nature, The Utility of Religion, Theism* (Amherst, NY: Prometheus Books).

Mitchel, Basil. 1993. "War and Friendship," in Kelly James Clark (ed.), *Philosophers Who Believe: The Spiritual Journeys of 11 Leading Thinkers* (Downers Grove, IL: InterVarsity Press).

Murray, Michael J. 2008. "Four Arguments that the Cognitive Psychology of Religion Undermines the Justification of Religious Belief," in J. Bulbulia, R. Sosis, E. Harris, R. Genet, C. Genet and K. Wyman (eds.), *The Evolution of Religion: Studies, Theories, and Critiques* (Santa Margarita: Collins Foundation Press).

Murray, Michael J. 2009. "Scientific Explanations of Religion and the Justification of Religious Belief," in J. Schloss and M. J. Murray (eds.), *The Believing Primate* (Oxford: Oxford University Press).

Murray, Michael J., and Lyn Moore. 2009. "Costly Signaling and the Origin of Religion," *Journal of Cognition and Culture*, 9: 225–45.

Nichols, Shaun. 2007. "Imagination and Immortality: Thinking of Me," *Synthese*, 159: 215–33.

Nola, Robert. 2013. "Do Naturalistic Explanations of Religious Beliefs Debunk Religion?" in Gregory W. Dawes and James Maclaurin (eds.), *A New Science of Religion* (New York and London: Routledge).

Nola, Robert. 2018. "Demystifying Religious Belief," in Hans van Eyghen, Rik Peels and Gijsbert van den Brink (eds.), *New Developments in the Cognitive Science of Religion* (Dordrecht: Springer).

Norenzayan, Ara. 2013. *Big Gods: How Religion Transformed Cooperation and Conflict* (Princeton and New Jersey: Princeton University Press).

O' Dwyer, Shaun. 2015. "Epistemic Elitism, Paternalism, and Confucian Democracy," *Dao*, 14: 33–54.

Okasha, Samir. 2013. "Biological Altruism." Accessed December 12, 2016. https://plato.stanford.edu/entries/altruism-biological/ - KinSelIncFit.

Oppy, Graham. 2006. *Arguing About Gods.* (Cambridge: Cambridge University Press).

Paley, William. 2006. *Natural Theology or Evidence for the Existence and Attributes of the Deity, Collected from the Appearances of Nature* (Oxford: Oxford University Press).

Palmer, Craig T., and Ryan O. Begley. 2015. "Costly Signaling Theory, Sexual Selection, and the Influence of Ancestors on Religious Behavior," in D. Jason Slone and James A. Van Slyke (eds.), *The Attraction of Religion: A New Evolutionary Psychology of Religion* (London: Bloomsbury Academic).

Papineau, David. 2007. "Naturalism," *The Stanford Encyclopedia of Philosophy* (Winter 2016 Edition).
Peels, Rik. 2017. "The Fundamental Argument Against Scientism," in Maarten Boudry and Massimo Pigliucci (eds.), *Science Unlimited? The Challenges of Scientism* (Chicago: Chicago University Press).
Persinger, Michael A. 1985. "Geophysical Variables and Behavior: XXX. Intense Paranormal Experiences Occur During Days of Quiet, Global, Geomagnetic Activity," *Perceptual and Motor Skills*, 61: 320–22.
Persinger, M. A., and S. Koren. 2005. "A Response to Granqvist et al. 'Sensed Presence and Mystical Experiences are Predicted by Suggestibility, Not by the Application of Transcranial Weak Magnetic Fields,'" *Neuroscience Letters*, 380: 346–47.
Philipse, Herman. 2012. *God in the Age of Science: A Critique of Religious Reason* (Oxford: Oxford University Press).
Phillips, Dewi Zephaniah. 1976. *Religion without Explanation* (Oxford: Blackwell).
Plantinga, Alvin. 1975. *God, Freedom and Evil* (London: Allen and Unwin).
Plantinga, Alvin. 1986. "Two Dozen (or so) Theistic Arguments," in Deane-Peter Baker (ed.), *Alvin Plantinga* (Cambridge: Cambridge University Press).
Plantinga, Alvin. 2000. *Warranted Christian Belief* (New York, NY: Oxford University Press).
Plantinga, Alvin. 2011. *Where the Conflict Really Lies: Science, Religion, and Naturalism* (Oxford: Oxford University Press).
Plato. 2006. "Laws. Book X." Accessed January 19, 2017. http://classics.mit.edu/Plato/laws.10.x.html.
Poston, Ted. no data. "Internalism and Externalism in Epistemology." Accessed August 16, 2019. https://www.iep.utm.edu/int-ext/.
Priest, Graham, and Fransesco Berto. 2013. "Dialetheism." Accessed March 15, 2016. http://plato.stanford.edu/archives/sum2013/entries/dialetheism/.
Randolph-Seng, Brandon, and Michael E. Nielsen. 2007. "Honesty: One Effect of Primed Religious Representations," *The International Journal for the Psychology of Religion*, 17: 303–15.
Richerson, Peter J., and Lesley Newson. 2008. "Is Religion Adaptive? Yes, No, Neutral, But Mostly, We Don't Know," in J. Schloss and M. J. Murray (eds.), *The Believing Primate. Scientific, Philosophical, and Theological Reflections on the Origin of Religion* (Oxford: Oxford University Press).

Roes, Frans L., and Michel Raymond. 2003. "Belief in Moralizing Gods," *Evolution and Human Behavior*, 24: 126–35.

Rosenberg, Alex. 1996. "A Field Guide to Recent Species of Naturalism," *The British Journal for the Philosophy of Science*, 47: 1–29.

Ross, H. 1998. "General Revelation: Nature's Testament," *Philosophia Christi*, 21: 9–16.

Rowe, William L. 1979. "The Problem of Evil and Some Varieties of Atheism," *American Philosophical Quarterly*: 335–41.

Ruffle, Bradley J., and Richard Sosis. 2005. "Cooperation and the In-Group Out-Group Bias: A Field Test on Israeli Kibbutz Members and City Residents," *Journal of Economic Behavior and Organization*, 60: 147–63.

Ruse, Michael, and Edward O. Wilson. 1986. "Moral Philosophy as Applied Science: A Darwinian Approach to the Foundations of Ethics," *Philosophy*, 61: 173–92.

Russell, Bertrand. 1957. *Why I Am Not a Christian* (New York: Simon and Schuster).

Saler, Benson. 1999. "Family Resemblance and the Definition of Religion," *Historical Reflections / Réflexions Historiques*, 25: 391–404.

Saroglou, Vassilis. 2012. "Is Religion Not Prosocial at All? Comment on Galen," *Psychological Bulletin*, 138: 907–12.

Shanks, N., and K. Green. 2011. "Intelligent Design in Theological Perspective," *Synthese*, 178 (2): 307–30.

Shariff, Azim F. 2015. "Does Religion Increase Moral Behavior?" *Current Opinion in Psychology*, 6: 108–13.

Shariff, Azim F., and Ara Norenzayan. 2011. "Mean Gods Make Good People: Different Views of God Predict Cheating Behavior," *The International Journal for the Psychology of Religion*, 21: 85–96.

Shariff, Azim F., Ara Norenzayan, and J. Henrich. 2009. "The Birth of High Gods: How the Cultural Evolution of Supernatural Policing Agents Influenced the Emergence of Complex, Cooperative Human Societies, Paving the Way for Civilization," in M. Schaller, A. Norenzayan, S. Heine, T. Yamagishi and T. Kameda (eds.), *Evolution, Culture and the Human Mind* (New York: Psychology Press).

Shaver, John, and Richard Sosis. 2014. "How Does Male Ritual Behavior Vary Across the Lifespan? An Examination of Fijian Kava Ceremonies," *Human Nature*, 25: 136–60.

Shermer, Michael. 2012. "Dr Michael Shermer | God Does NOT Exist." Accessed August 28, 2017. https://www.youtube.com/watch?v=0pOI2YvVuuE.

Slone, D. Jason. 2004. *Theological Incorrectness: Why Religious People Believe What They Shouldn't* (Oxford: Oxford University Press).

Slone, D. Jason, and James A. Van Slyke. 2015a. *The Attraction of Religion: A New Evolutionary Psychology of Religion* (London: Bloomsbury Academic).

Slone, Jason, and James A. Van Slyke. 2015b. "Introduction: Connecting Religion, Sex, and Evolution," in Jason Slone and James A. Van Slyke (eds.), *The Attraction of Religion: A New Evolutionary Psychology of Religion* (London: Bloomsbury Academic).

Sober, E. 1981. "The Principle of Parsimony," *British Journal for the Philosophy of Science*, 32 (2): 145–56.

Sober, Elliott. 2001. "What Is the Problem of Simplicity?" in Arnold Zellner, Hugo A. Keuzenkampf, Michael McAleer, Arnold Zellner, Hugo A. Keuzenkampf and Michael McAleer (eds.), *Simplicity, Inference and Modelling: Keeping It Sophisticatedly Simple* (Cambridge: Cambridge University Press).

Sørensen, Jesper. 2005. "Religion in Mind: A Review Article of the Cognitive Science of Religion," *Numen*, 52: 465–94.

Sosis, Richard. 2000. "Costly Signalling and Torch Fishing on Ifaluk Atoll," *Evolution and Human Behavior*, 21: 223–44.

Sosis, Richard. 2005. "Does Religion Promote Trust? The Role of Signaling, Reputation, and Punishment," *Interdisciplinary Journal of Research in Religion*, 1.

Sosis, R., and E. R. Bressler. 2003. "Cooperation and Commune Longevity: A Test of the Costly Signaling Theory of Religion," *Cross-Cultural Research*, 37: 211–39.

Sosis, Richard, and Jordan Kiper. 2014. "Religion Is More Than Belief: What Evolutionary Theories of Religion Tell Us About Religious Commitment," in Michael Bergman and Patrick Kain (eds.), *Challenges to Religion and Morality: Disagreements and Evolution* (Oxford: Oxford University Press).

Sperber, Dan. 1997. "Intuitive and Reflective Beliefs," *Mind and Language*, 12: 67–83.

Sperber, Dan, and Lawrence Hirschfeld. 1999. "Culture, Cognition, and Evolution," in R. A. Wilson and F. C. Keil (eds.), *MIT Encyclopedia of the Cognitive Sciences* (Cambridge: The MIT Press), 111–32.

Street, Sharon. 2006. "A Darwinian Dilemma for Realist Theories of Value," *Philosophical Studies*, 127: 109–66.
Swann Jr., W. B., J. Jetten, Á. Gómez, H. Whitehouse, and B. Bastian 2012. "When Group Membership Gets Personal: A Theory of Identity Fusion," *Psychological Review*, 119 (3): 441.
Swinburne, Richard. 1993. *The Coherence of Theism* (Oxford: Clarendon Press and Oxford University Press).
Swinburne, Richard. 2004. *The Existence of God* (Oxford: Oxford University Press).
Tangney, June Price. 2001. "Self-Conscious Emotions: The Self as a Moral Guide," in A. Tesser, D. A. Stapel and J. V. Wood (eds.), *Self and Motivation: Emerging Psychological Perspectives* (Washington, DC: American Psychological Association).
Thomson, Andy. 2009. "Why We Believe in Gods—Andy Thomson—American Atheists 09," Accessed August 28, 2017. https://www.youtube.com/watch?v=1iMmvu9eMrg.
Thornhill-Miller, Branden, and Peter Millican. 2015. "The Common-Core/Diversity Dilemma: Revisions of Humean thought, New Empirical Research, and the Limits of Rational Religious Belief," *European Journal for Philosophy of Religion*, 7: 1–49.
Thurow, Joshua. 2013. "Does Cognitive Science Show Belief in God to be Irrational? The Epistemic Consequences of the Cognitive Science of Religion," *International Journal for Philosophy of Religion*, 74 (1): 77–98.
Tillich, Paul Johannes Oskar. 1953. *Systematic Theology* (London: Nisbet).
Trivers, Robert. 1971. "The Evolution of Reciprocal Altruism," *Quarterly Review of Biology*, 46: 35–57.
Tucker, Aviezer. 2003. "The Epistemic Significance of Consensus," *Inquiry*, 46: 501–21.
Turiel, Elliot. 2002. *The Culture of Morality: Social Development, Context and Conflict* (Cambridge: Cambridge University Press).
Van den Brink, Gijsbert. 2015. "Openbaring Overbodig? Een verkenning van enkele hedendaagse CSR-verklaringen van het ontstaan van godsdienstigheid," in Ad de Bruijne, Hans Burger and Dolf te Velde (eds.), *Weergaloze kennis. Opstellen over Jezus Christus, Openbaring en Schrift, Katholiciteit en Kerkaangeboden aan prof. dr. B. Kamphuis* (Zoetermeer: Boekencentrum).
Van den Brink, Gijsbert. 2018. *Reformed Theology and Evolutionary Theory* (Grand Rapids Michigan: Eerdmans).

Van Elk, Michiel. 2013. "Paranormal Believers Are More Prone to Illusory Agency Detection Than Skeptics," *Consciousness and Cognition*, 22: 1041–46.
Van Elk, Michiel, and André Aleman. 2017. "Brain Mechanisms in Religion and Spirituality: An Integrative Predictive Processing Framework," *Neuroscience & Biobehavioral Reviews*, 73: 359–78.
Van Eyghen, Hans. 2016. "Two Types of 'Explaining Away' Arguments in the Cognitive Science of Religion," *Zygon*, 51: 966–82.
Van Eyghen, Hans. 2018a. "Predictive Coding and Religious Belief," *Filosofia Unisinos*, 19: 302–10.
Van Eyghen, Hans. 2018b. "The Retreat Argument," *Heythrop Journal*: 497–508.
Van Eyghen, Hans. 2018c. "Spirit Beliefs Debunked?," *Science, Religion, and Culture*, 5 (1): 73–82.
Van Eyghen, Hans. 2019. "Is supernatural belief unreliably formed?," *International Journal for Philosophy of Religion*, 85 (2): 1–24.
Van Eyghen, Hans, Rik Peels, and Gijsbert van den Brink. 2018. "Introduction: The Cognitive Science of Religion, Philosophy and Theology: A Survey of the Issues," in Hans van Eyghen, Rik Peels and Gijsbert van den Brink (eds.), *New Developments in the Cognitive Science of Religion—The Rationality of Religious Belief* (Cham: Springer).
Van Fraassen, Bas Cornelis. 1980. *The Scientific Image* (Oxford: Clarendon).
Van Fraassen, Bas Cornelis. 1989. *Laws and Symmetry* (Oxford and New York: Clarendon Press).
Van Inwagen, Peter. 2009. "Explaining Belief in the Supernatural. Some thoughts on Paul Bloom's 'Religious Belief as Evolutionary Accident'," in J. Schloss and M. J. Murray (eds.), *The Believing Primate: Scientific, Philosophical, and Theological Reflections on the Origin of Religion* (New York: Oxford University Press).
Van Leeuwen, Neil, and Michiel van Elk. 2018. "Seeking the Supernatural: The Interactive Religious Experience Model," *Religion, Brain & Behavior*, 9 (3): 221–251.
Van Woudenberg, René, and Hans van Eyghen. 2017. "Most Peers Don't Believe It, Hence It Is Probably False," *European Journal for Philosophy of Religion*, 9: 87–112.
Watts, Joseph, Simon J. Greenhill, Quentin D. Atkinson, Thomas E. Currie, Joseph Bulbulia, and Russell D. Gray. 2015. "Broad Supernatural Punishment but Not Moralizing High Gods Precede the Evolution of

Political Complexity in Austronesia," in *Proceedings of the Royal Society B.*, 20142556. The Royal Society.

Wegner, D. M. 2002. *The Illusion of Conscious Will* (Cambridge, MA: MIT Press).

White, Claire. 2017. "What the Cognitive Science of Religion Is (and Is Not)," in Aaron W. Hughes (ed.), *Theory in a Time of Excess—The Case of the Academic Study of Religion* (London: Equinox Publishing).

Whitehouse, Harvey. 2004. *Modes of Religiosity: A Cognitive Theory of Religious Transmission* (Lanham: Rowman Altamira).

Whitehouse, Harvey, and Jonathan A. Lanman. 2014. "The Ties That Bind Us," *Current Anthropology*, 55: 674–95.

Whitehouse, Harvey, Brian McQuinn, Michael Buhrmester, and William B. Swann. 2014. "Brothers in Arms: Libyan Revolutionaries Bond Like Family," *Proceedings of the National Academy of Sciences*, 111: 17783–85.

Whitehouse, Harvey, William Swann, Gordon Ingram, Karolina Prochownik, Jonathan Lanman, Timothy M. Waring, Karl Frost, Douglas Jones, Zoey Reeve, and Dominic Johnson. 2013. "Three Wishes for the World (with comment)," *Cliodynamics: The Journal of Theoretical and Mathematical History*, 64.

Whitehouse, Harvey, Pieter Francois, Patrick E. Savage, Thomas E. Currie, Kevin C. Feeney, Enrico Cioni, Rosalind Purcell, Robert M. Ross, Jennifer Larson, John Baines, Barend Ter Haar, Alan Covey, and Peter Turchin. 2019. "Complex Societies Precede Moralizing Gods throughout World History," *Nature*, 568 (7751): 226.

Wilkins, John S., and Paul E. Griffiths. 2013. "Evolutionary Debunking Arguments in Three Domains: Fact, Value, and Religion," in Gregory Dawes and James Maclaurin (eds.), *A New Science of Religion* (London: Routledge).

Wittgenstein, Ludwig. 1958. *Philosophical Investigations* (Oxford: Basil Blackwell).

Xygalatas, Dimitris, Panagiotis Mitkidis, Ronald Fischer, Paul Reddish, Joshua Skewes, Armin W. Geertz, Andreas Roepstorff, and Joseph Bulbulia. 2013. "Extreme Rituals Promote Prosociality," *Psychological Science*, xx: 1–4.

Zagzebski, Linda. 2011. "Epistemic Self-Trust and the Consensus Gentium Argument," in Kelly James Clark and Raymond J. Van Arragon (eds.), *Evidence and Religious Belief* (Oxford: Oxford University Press).

Index

adaptationist theory   14, 20, 24, 31, 43, 70, 71, 142, 146
afterlife   31, 34–5, 110
Alston, William   91–2, 95, 145, 167 n.42, 174 n.20
animism   8, 36
argument from religious experiences   114–17
atheism   2, 74, 130, 136, 139, 151 n.22, 162 n.48, 175 n.27, 31

Barrett, Justin   29, 36–8, 41, 43, 62, 63, 71, 76, 78, 87, 94, 97, 104, 107, 110, 118, 150 n.2, 155 n.70, 155 n.72, 160 n.16, 168 n.56
Bering, Jesse   15–18, 22, 34–5, 40–1, 62, 78, 107
Bloom, Paul   33, 62, 69–70, 97 168 n.56.
Boyer, Pascal   23, 30–1, 33, 41–3, 51–4, 63, 107, 154 n.57, 157 n.125, 157 n.127, 158 n.26, 159 n.40, 160 n.12, 161 n.27
Buddhism   6, 48, 67, 92, 133, 168
by-product   31

Christianity   5–10, 22, 45, 55, 58, 59, 68, 69, 71, 72, 73, 75, 77, 78, 92, 104, 130, 132, 133, 136, 138, 141, 150 n.7, 150 n.15, 160 n.16, 163 n.53, 164 n.64, 167 n.33, 168 n.55, 170 n.76, 174 n.17
Clark, Kelly   71, 78, 83, 87, 150 n.2, 150 n.3, 155 n.72, 162 n.48, 163 n.51, 164 n.69, 164 n.70, 177 n.53
consensus gentium argument   130–9
cosmological argument   77, 122–4, 144

De Cruz, Helen   67, 73–5, 77, 85, 144, 159 n.1, 161 n.26, 163 n.59, 166 n.20
design argument   85, 123–4, 144, 164 n.67. 172 n.30
dialetheism   68, 161 n.37
dualism   31, 33–4, 35, 154 n.59

generality problem for reliabilism   166 n.27
god, definition of   103, 130
Gray, Kurt   38–40, 107–9, 170 n.72
Guthrie, Stewart   36, 43, 106, 107–10, 170 n.71, 170 n.79

Hinduism   7, 9–10, 47–8, 59, 92, 103, 104, 138, 159 n.42, 168 n.55
hyperactive agency detection device   36–8

Islam   6, 104, 130

James, William   2–3, 149 n.14, 168 n.51
Johnson, Dominic   15–18, 151 n.9
Judaism   75, 168 n.55

Kelemen, Deborah   32–3, 37

Lawson, E. Thomas   14
Luhrmann, Tanya   14, 125, 159 n.41

McCauley, Robert   14

naturalism   2, 109, 110, 122, 126, 129–30, 131, 132, 133, 136, 140, 143, 144, 145, 146, 163 n.56, 173 n.2, 173 n.3, 176 n.48

natural theology   90, 122, 135, 144, 166 n.20
neuroscience of religious experiences   54–6
Norenzayan, Ara   17, 22–3, 161 n.23

parsimony, principle of   117, 120–1, 143, 172 n.23, 177 n.54
Persinger, Michael   55–6, 58, 120, 122, 124, 126, 127
Plantinga, Alvin   2, 71, 78, 87, 162 n.47, 163 n.51, 163 n.58, 164 n.69, 173 n.3
predictive coding   54, 56–9, 120, 122, 123

Reformed Epistemology   163 n.51, 166 n.17
religious belief, definition of   6–11
religious experience   10–11, 45, 54–60, 64, 91, 94
ritual   6, 7, 11, 13, 14, 25, 26, 45–54, 59, 61–2, 64, 65, 67, 69, 73–5, 77, 79, 101, 147, 157 n.1, 159 n.40, 159 n.42, 161 n.26, 163 n.59, 164 n.64

sensus divinitatis   71–2, 78, 162 n.47, 163 n.51, 164 n.69

Sperber, Dan   28–9, 154 n.57
spirits   6, 7, 9, 10, 37, 59, 92, 93, 130, 136, 150 n.9, 157 n.126, 173 n.5
supernatural being, definition of   8–9
supernatural belief, definition of   7–10
Swinburne, Richard   114–17, 121, 136

teleology   31–3, 35, 70, 85, 144
theism   5, 63, 70, 77, 82, 83, 85, 99, 101, 114, 118, 119, 121, 130, 137, 138, 141, 142, 150 nn.3, 4, 151 n.22, 163 n.56, 164 n.68, 176 nn.52, 53
theory of mind   14, 27, 37–8, 40–1, 70, 78, 82, 86, 97, 99, 103, 104

Van Inwagen, Peter   69–71, 150 n.6, 154 n.59
Visala, Aku   14, 63, 83–5, 99, 118–19, 149 n.15, 160 n.20, 176 n.53

Wegner, Daniel   1, 38–40, 107–9, 170 n.72
Whitehouse, Harvey   19, 20, 23–4, 49–51, 74–5, 159 n.40

www.ingramcontent.com/pod-product-compliance
Lightning Source LLC
Chambersburg PA
CBHW070637300426
44111CB00013B/2148